How to survive working in a church school

A guide for all teachers and support staff in Church of England and Church in Wales schools

CONTENTS

Foreword by the Right Revd John Pritchard, former Bishop of Oxford and former Chair, Church of England Board of Education		Page 2
Introduction		Page 7
Chapter 1	*Help! What Am I Doing Here?*	Page 10
Chapter 2	*About the Christian Church and Anglicanism*	Page 18
Chapter 3	*The Background and History of Church Education in England and Wales*	Page 24
Chapter 4	*What is a Church School and How is it Different?*	Page 32
Chapter 5	*Christian Spirituality and Ethos*	Page 44
Chapter 6	*The Seasons and Traditions of the Anglican Communion*	Page 56
Chapter 7	*Who's Who*	Page 62
Chapter 8	*Guidance for Praying and Suggestions for Prayers*	Page 66
A Glossary of Christian Terms		Page 74
Further Reading and Resources		Page 82

FOREWORD

Not long ago my wife and I were with our five-year-old granddaughter when she went to school for the first time. Off we all went – her parents, grandparents, little brother, and a collection of other children and parents we picked up on the way. Our granddaughter was completely unfazed by all this concern and chatted with her little friends about their new shoes as they waited in line to disappear into the educational system for the next sixteen years. But we were quite emotional. This was the start of a major process of formation that would have untold results. How would she be shaped by it? How would she cope with the pressures? How would she handle the inevitable broken friendships and possible cyber-bullying and the vagaries of the exam system? How would this five-year-old emerge at twenty-one?

For every parent – and grandparent – the stakes in education are high. We're all deeply committed; we all have definite views. And the people at the sharp end, those who are expected to deliver a first-rate educational experience to our much-loved children, are the hundreds of thousands of highly motivated people who teach, support and facilitate in our schools.

It's very good, therefore, to have a book dedicated to helping those who teach in Church of England and Church in Wales schools to reflect on the unique gift that such schools offer. The Church, after all, was responsible for starting a national network of schools back in 1811, long before the state became involved in education. Even now the C of E oversees a quarter of the country's primary schools and hundreds of secondaries. It is the largest provider of academies and completely committed to providing high-quality, all-round education to nearly a million children.

President John F. Kennedy once said: "Our progress as a nation can be no swifter than our progress in education. The human mind is our fundamental resource." Agreed. But we are more than minds. The human spirit is also our fundamental resource. So it's worth thinking about – as this book does so well – what makes a church school distinctive. We will all agree with the poet W.B. Yeats, who said: "Education is not the filling of a bucket but the lighting of a fire." But what does that mean in a church school, and how does that affect those who work there?

I dare to suggest that there are four things that have to stand out in the way a church school approaches its task.

FOREWORD

The first is its emphasis on every child being made in the image of God

All schools put the child centre-stage but church schools have a particular motivation for that – they see each child as uniquely God-made and God-loved. John Milton wrote about "a complete and generous education", which would fit a child "to perform justly, skilfully and magnanimously" in society. It's been said that our educational system sometimes seems to be intent on producing people whose bodies are there only to get their heads to a meeting. Our value does not lie only in the size of our brain or our potential as a contributor to the country's GDP. Every child has an extraordinary all-round potential, because every child is made in the image of God – and you can't give anyone higher value than that.

The second foundation undergirding a church school is the life, death and new life of Jesus of Nazareth

That narrative gives a school its values and priorities – for example, the primacy of love, the importance of forgiveness, the value of those who are vulnerable and marginalised, the necessity of justice, the call of compassion, and so on. Moreover, the compelling narrative of Jesus has shaped our culture in ways we may now try to disown, but it reaches deeply into our common life through the influence it's had on the legal system, parliamentary democracy, science, healthcare, education, philanthropy, the arts and much more. The writer H.G. Wells, an unbeliever, wrote: "I have to say, as a historian, that this penniless preacher from Galilee is irrevocably the centre of history." The life of Jesus is a magnificent resource for a church school, the centrepiece of the whole structure.

Church schools are also committed to being community builders

Again, as with the value of each child, this is not unique. However, Christians are well practised in understanding how community works. Whereas successive governments, pundits and opinion formers throw around the importance of community, we've been getting on and doing it for two thousand years, putting people together from all kinds of backgrounds in love and mutual support, and going out and serving the wider community in the name of Christ. These "communities of

Trinity Academy, Halifax

grace" are rich in love, trust, hospitality, openness, generosity and hope, and schools are very often at the core of such church communities. Children learn what it means to love our neighbour – and even, hopefully, to love our enemy.

The fourth foundation stone underlying church schools is the importance of spiritual space

In a noisy, distracted and bewildered culture, spiritual formation is a core task of a rounded education. There's a desperate need for stillness. Church schools have the opportunity to nurture children in the arts of prayer, reflection and worship. There will be high-quality RS, including other faiths, and maybe some Godly Play, or regular visitors from an Open the Book team. Perhaps there will be a connection with Messy Church and other children's groups run in the local church or in the school itself. There'll be visits to churches and other sacred places, and maybe an introduction to pilgrimage. In all sorts of ways there'll be an experience of spiritual space as an integral part of a whole and healthy life.

This book gives a very helpful glimpse into the ethos and practices of church schools. It doesn't assume more faith than we have. It doesn't assume that all church schools are wonderful. But it does set out some guidelines for the journey, a journey we can all relish.

Including, I can happily report, my little granddaughter.

The Right Reverend John Pritchard

John Pritchard was Bishop of Jarrow between 2002 and 2007, and Bishop of Oxford from 2007 until 2014. He was Chair of the Church of England's Board of Education and Episcopal Spokesperson on Education in the House of Lords.

Q&A with the Archbishop of Wales, Dr Barry Morgan, in the Faith Garden at Peterston Super Ely C in W School

Trinity Academy

INTRODUCTION

How to Survive Working in a Church School is for anyone who works in a church school, or who is thinking of applying for a job in one. Although church schools have a strong track record and are generally great places to work, you may want to find out more in order to explore what it means for you personally, or you may find aspects of the school and its Christian ethos confusing or even concerning. So this book is designed to answer some of your questions and to allay some of your concerns.

Is this book just for practising Christians and churchgoers?

Definitely not. This book is for *everyone* who works in a church school. Most of us are not experts – we're just doing the best we know how. This book aims to be real and to deal with issues in a down-to-earth way. Think of it as a practical guide to surviving (and we hope thriving) in a church school. We'll try to fill any gaps in knowledge you may have about the Church and its schools, so that the next time a child asks you an awkward question – "Does everyone who doesn't believe go to hell?", or "What did Jesus mean by loving your neighbour?" – you don't feel put on the spot. Even if you don't know the answer yourself, at the very least this book should give you the confidence to find out more, and know where to start looking for answers.

So is this book just for teachers?

Again, no. Or, to put it another way, everybody who works in a church school is in some way a teacher. Whether you are the cleaner, headteacher, teaching assistant, caretaker, cook or receptionist, the children and young people will look up to you in ways that you're probably not aware of. Children are natural copycats, they miss nothing, and are affected in some way by every encounter. So every individual who works in a church school in some way represents what the school is all about.

How to use this book

This book is designed for a wide variety of readers, some of whom will be very familiar with Christianity, the Anglican Communion,[1] and its practices and traditions. For others, however, these things may be shrouded in mystery. So you are invited to read it in whatever way suits your needs. Chapter Five, for example, deals with the subject of "Christian spirituality and ethos". If you don't feel ready to tackle this, or if your immediate need is more practical (such as looking for a prayer to use for the end of term, or wanting to understand the role of a deacon), you will find quick-reference guides near the back of the book, while Chapter Two introduces the Christian faith and explains a bit about terms such as "Anglicanism" and "Protestantism", and looks at how the Church of England and Church in Wales fit into the picture.

You will also find a useful glossary of terms at the back of the book, along with further reading and resources to enable you to explore more deeply.

That said, please don't dismiss the theology and spirituality that you'll find in the book. Although you might need to find a quiet place and devote a bit of time to it for reflection, Christian spirituality is the heart and soul of every church school, and everyone who works in one – of whatever faith background or none – will find that understanding more about it will enrich them – not just in their work, but in their whole life.

Time to think and reflect

The pace of life seems to be going one way – faster – and most of us don't get much time to stop and think. The technology that was supposed to make life easier only seems to have made it busier. In a church school it is important that everybody gets a chance to stop, catch their breath, reflect on what they're doing and try to understand in a deeper way what the mission of the school is and the part they play in it as individuals. There will be a space in each chapter for reflection and prayer. To use this resource fully and meaningfully, it will be helpful to set aside some time for it. If you don't feel comfortable with Christian prayer, please feel free to adapt the prayers to your own tradition, if appropriate, or simply use them for reflection.

Above all, we hope that this book reassures you that what you find in your church school is relevant to you and your life, and that you have a meaningful and important role to play and a great deal to contribute to the life of the school and everyone in it, whatever your own background and outlook.

A NOTE ABOUT USING THE BIBLE

Throughout this book you will find references to passages from the Bible. As it is the main source of Christian teaching and scripture, a basic understanding of the Bible is important. It's worth getting hold of a copy and learning to navigate your way around it. A member of the clergy or one of your work colleagues should be able to point you in the right direction, or you can find plenty of Bible resources online.[2]

Just to get you started, the Bible, which usually comes in the form of a single volume, is sub-divided into two main parts, known as the Old Testament (the history of the Jewish people up until the birth of Jesus) and the New Testament (which recounts Jesus' life on earth, his death and resurrection, and the life of the early Church). The Old and New Testaments are sub-divided further into "books". Of these, the four Gospels – Matthew, Mark, Luke and John – are particularly important, and are an extremely good place to start to explore the Christian faith and the teachings and life of Christ.

Each of these books of the Bible is divided into "chapters" and "verses". If you want to look up Matthew 22:36-40, for example, you need to find the twenty-second chapter of Matthew, then look up verses thirty-six to forty.

INTRODUCTION

These verses are actually an extremely good starting point, as they form the bedrock of Jesus' teaching:

> "Teacher, which commandment in the law is the greatest?" He said to him, "'You shall love the Lord your God with all your heart, and with all your soul, and with all your mind.' This is the greatest and first commandment. And a second is like it: 'You shall love your neighbour as yourself.' On these two commandments hang all the law and the prophets."
>
> *Matthew 22:36-40*

Take a bit of time to reflect on these verses, and how they might apply to situations in your life and your work in the school.

---

1 For more about what this term means, see p. 21.

2 For example, you can find several translations of the Bible at www.crosswalk.com. Of the various translations that are available, the NRSV (New Revised Standard Version) is the one used officially in the Anglican Communion and is the best starting point.

CHAPTER 1

Help! What Am I Doing Here?

So you work in a church school. Whether you've been there for ten days or ten years, there will probably have been moments when you've wondered, "What on earth am I doing here?" You may be very happy in the school – it's got a great ethos, a real family atmosphere and a sense of respect among staff and students – but equally there may well have been times when you have found yourself mystified by some of the "churchy" stuff, or daunted by the prospect of working in a Christian environment, and may not have had the confidence to ask a question or express your opinion about something.

Here are just some of the concerns you may have raised or questions you may have asked:

I'm a practising Christian and churchgoer, but to be honest I find the idea of working in a Christian environment daunting

The first thing to say is that you're certainly not alone! For many people, faith is compartmentalised – confined to church on Sunday morning – and it would be unthinkable to carry it through the rest of the week, let alone to their place of work. If this describes you, it would be a good idea to spend some time reflecting on and praying about what your faith means to you. Be honest, and don't put yourself under pressure. Where are you on your journey, and where do you see yourself heading? Give some thought to the important things in your life – your family, friends, health, career – and ask how your faith life affects and is affected by each of these.

Nobody in any environment should ever feel that their faith has to stand up to scrutiny from anyone else – be they other staff, the school chaplain, parents or even the students! At the end of the day, you have a unique "faith print" and you are on your own journey, and whether or not you are a good Christian is solely between you and God. Nobody else should or could judge you as a Christian. What they can do is to offer support, guidance and, when you seek it, advice and suggestions.

All the same, working in a Christian environment is a very good opportunity to deepen your faith. It would be a mistake to assume that means that you have to adhere rigidly to a fixed belief system – far from it. Rather, through exploring, questioning, challenging and even doubting, you should find ways to make the Christian faith more relevant, meaningful and fulfilling. And if all that sounds rather egocentric, actually the opposite is true. We find true personal fulfilment through learning to love God and serve others (Matthew 22:36-40). This is one of the wonderful paradoxes of Christianity, which can only be learnt through first-hand experience. In self-giving and serving others, we become personally richer and more fulfilled than we ever could do in putting our own needs and desires first and foremost. How wonderful to have an opportunity to explore that and live it out in a school environment, where young lives and future generations are formed!

> **PAUSE FOR THOUGHT**
>
> Where do your sympathies for the school's Christian ethos begin and end? What drew you to the school in the first place? Be honest – if it's the wage or working conditions, that's okay. We will be looking at this in more depth, but at this stage it's helpful to start thinking about it.

I'm not from a church background and I'm not always sure whether I fit in

First, and importantly, don't forget that you have been given your job because your skills, experience and qualities make you right for the role, regardless of your own background, religious faith or personal outlook. Christians believe that each and every one of us has God-given skills and talents, and that each individual should be valued as such. What's more, each and every one of us is God's unique creation, so the emphasis should be on respecting and celebrating difference, rather than discriminating against anyone who doesn't conform or fit in. You should be made to feel that you are a valued member of the school community because of, not despite, your unique circumstances.

It's probably also true to say that at some level you will have sympathy for what the school stands for. Indeed, there aren't many people who work in church schools who are anti-Christian, or anti-religious – that would be a bit strange. So this is an opportunity to explore how you can fulfil your potential through your work and, in turn, how your job can enrich you and your life.

I come from a Christian background and I used to go to church when I was a child, but now I'm just keeping up appearances

The spiritual life is a journey, and most people who are honest about their faith will tell you that there are times of doubt and drift. It's normal, and you should not be judged by anyone on that score. Jesus was clear about that when he said: "Do not judge, and you will not be judged" (Luke 6:37). So rather than living with a vague uneasiness or sense of not fitting in, or even hiding any doubts or concerns, use the opportunity to revisit your religious heritage and give some thought to what it means to you now as an adult. Be honest about those aspects of the faith that may have led you to lose heart, and what you still find meaningful and helpful. You might want to ask someone, such as the school chaplain or a colleague, to work through some issues with you. You are, after all, in the best possible environment for this kind of enquiry, so use the resources at your disposal to the full!

> Doubt is not the opposite of faith; it is one element of faith.
>
> *Paul Tillich, philosopher and theologian*

I'm from another faith tradition – am I allowed to practise my own faith?

The Church emphatically believes in respecting and celebrating other faiths, and there should be a healthy level of enquiry and dialogue between all the faiths that are represented in the school and wider community.[1] So you should not only be allowed, but actively encouraged, to be open about your own traditions, values, customs and practices, and enabled to practise your faith in any way that's appropriate. If you have a particular requirement that needs to be specially accommodated, that is obviously a matter of negotiation with the headteacher and governors. What is asked of you is that you are in turn respectful of and engaged with the school's Christian values and ethos.

Sowerby Village CE (VC) Primary School

INTERVIEW – THE HISTORY TEACHER

When I first started working here seven years ago, I was asked the question about how, as a Muslim, I would feel working in a Christian environment. I felt then, and I feel now, that you're still going to have the same values. In this school, those values – Empathy, Honesty, Respect and Responsibility – were set out from the get go. So for me, when I have a conversation with a student, they are always relevant. For example, if I'm teaching about the history of slavery, or modern-day sex slavery, I'll look at the subject in light of empathy and respect.

Charity is one of the Five Pillars of Islam, so I have in the past been involved in the school's Charity Committee. I had to take a break from it when I got married and had my first child, but I'm planning to get involved again, and I'm happy that I can be true to my Muslim faith in this context.

When I say the Academy prayer, I do address the prayer to God, but I don't read the part at the end about the Father, the Son and the Holy Spirit. I never feel that anyone judges me – I think people respect that it's not part of my faith tradition.

Shabana Quassim, Second in the Department of Humanities, Trinity Academy, Halifax

CHAPTER 1

> "We have a number of children of different faiths. Some take part in a different form of worship, although there is no sense in which they are left out or marginalised. It's interesting to see that the children's friendship groups aren't necessarily aligned along religious lines, but they are really respectful of one another. I find that very encouraging."
>
> *Vicky Furnandiz, Assistant Head, Sowerby Village CE (VC) Primary School*

I'm not sure I can always live up to expectations in a church school

It needs to be said that, like any school, a church school expects those who work in it not to undermine its particular values or ethos in any way. That applies to both students and staff and, indeed, should be written into your contract – so there should be no surprise there. Indeed, it's not just the Church that would take this view – any school would expect an appropriate level of conduct from their staff. As we saw in the Introduction, whatever your role, you are a role model and an example for the students, whether or not you are aware of it.

If you have any doubts or questions, or feel judged or unable to meet the expected standards in any way, you are in an excellent place to seek guidance or counselling.

So often I see people who call themselves Christians behaving in ways I don't consider very Christian

It's worth remembering that, like any organisation or institution, the Church is made up of individual human beings, who are not exempt from human weakness, frailty and sin. That doesn't mean that they can't be great role models for the students and other staff. On the contrary, we learn about ourselves through our mistakes and misdemeanours – just as long as we don't keep repeating them!

No matter what your circumstances, background or role in the school, you should be encouraged to become a full, active participant in the life of the school. That might mean challenging the school as an institution, and the individuals who work there, to live up to their Christian standards and ideals. Each individual has so much God-given potential and it is a lifetime's work to fulfil it. A church school should provide fertile soil for that kind of growth.

So if you are aware that someone is behaving or has behaved in a way that you don't think is compatible with your understanding of Christian behaviour, think how you can challenge it. That doesn't necessarily mean shouting about it or running to the authorities. It could mean taking that person aside for a quiet word. Following the example of Jesus, Christians try to act with love and compassion in all things at all times. So what, in this instance, do you think Jesus would do about the situation?

13

I'm a Christian, but I feel awkward talking about or demonstrating my faith

There is no need to feel you should preach or convert other people to the Christian way of thinking. But neither should Christianity be a taboo subject – far from it! Too often we find it embarrassing or awkward to talk about our faith and what it means for us. As ever, Jesus provides us with the best advice. When he was preparing his disciples for their mission, sending them out to proclaim the good news, he issued some stark warnings about how difficult it would be. But couched in the midst of it are some wonderful words of reassurance:

> Do not worry about how you are to speak or what you are to say; for what you are to say will be given to you at that time; for it is not you who speak, but the Spirit of your Father speaking through you.
>
> *Matthew 10:19-20*

It's clear that if we are open to God in our lives we will be guided and supported. That, indeed, is the wonderful thing about faith – we're not on our own!

Wouldn't we be better just forgetting about religion and sticking to teaching?

Perhaps – if teaching were all that people needed to find happiness and fulfilment. Knowledge is a truly wonderful thing, but without wisdom it is meaningless. Christians believe that wisdom comes through deepening our relationship with God and learning to love one another. We do this by following the example of Jesus Christ. These are routes to real, lasting happiness and peace which will enrich our lives and sustain us as individuals and communities. If we can somehow impart these values to the next generation, that's truly wonderful – for young people, for ourselves, for our communities and for the future of humanity.

> The aim of education is the knowledge not of fact but of values.
>
> *William Ralph Inge (1860 – 1954), Dean of St Paul's Cathedral*

Sowerby Village CE (VC) Primary School

CHAPTER 1

What's the appeal of Christianity?

It's very hard if not impossible to put into words, but many people who live committed religious lives are kept going because they have from time to time experienced moments of insight into God's love. Although these moments are rare in the blur of everyday life, when they happen they are very powerful experiences, and generations of men and women of faith have tried to describe them. One of the things people describe is that everything becomes simpler and clearer, and we are no longer concerned by those things that don't matter. One of the greatest mystics was an Englishwoman called Julian of Norwich, who lived in the plague-devastated years of the fourteenth century. She is known for many wonderful sayings, including:

> All shall be well, and all shall be well, and all manner of thing shall be well.
>
> *Julian of Norwich*
> *Fourteenth-century mystic and theologian*

This is the lovely vision and expression of faith which Christians want to share with other people.

Trinity Academy

POINTS TO REMEMBER

- You are entitled to feel *at home* in your school – the governors appointed you, they want you there.

- None of us is a saint – we just do our best to live what we think is a good life.

- The Christian Church is a human organisation – people make mistakes and Christians don't always behave as you might expect, but they are also capable of great goodness and kindness.

POINTS FOR PERSONAL REFLECTION OR GROUP DISCUSSION

- Think back to when you were appointed to the school – what led you to apply?

- Think about your own experience of faith, whether you are from a religious background or not. What does it mean to you now? What part would you like faith to play in your life from now on?

- How do you view the Christian Church? What aspects of it do you regard as negative? Do you see these in your day-to-day experience in the school? If so, how might you challenge them?

- Think about some positive aspects of the Church – for example, its educational and charitable work, both at home and in the Third World. In what way do you feel you could contribute?

REFLECTION

God has created me to do Him some definite service. He has committed some work to me which He has not committed to another. I have my mission – I never may know it in this life, but I shall be told it in the next. Somehow I am necessary for His purposes, as necessary in my place as an Archangel in his – if, indeed, I fail, He can raise another, as He could make the stones children of Abraham. Yet I have a part in this great work; I am a link in a chain, a bond of connexion between persons. He has not created me for naught. I shall do good, I shall do His work; I shall be an angel of peace, a preacher of truth in my own place, while not intending it, if I do but keep His commandments and serve Him in my calling.

John Henry Newman
Catholic cardinal and theologian

---

[1] "Learning about religion" and "learning from religion" are the two Attainment (or Assessment) Objectives for RS in all schools. All schools should follow the guidelines for teaching Religious Studies set out in a Locally Agreed Syllabus. These will normally expect that students learn *about* the six major world faiths (Judaism, Christianity, Islam, Hinduism, Buddhism, Sikhism). They may also learn about other minority religions, and atheist/non-religious world views. The second Assessment Objective ("learning from") is designed to encourage students to reflect on their own spirituality in the light of these various religious expressions.

Trinity Academy

CHAPTER 2

About the Christian Church and Anglicanism

The Christian faith

The chances are that a sign outside your school indicates that it is a Church in Wales (possibly abbreviated to "C in W") or Church of England ("C of E") school. This means that your school is Christian in the Protestant tradition known as Anglicanism. This chapter explains some of these terms in a very basic way, although of course it can only really scratch the surface.

All this is simply orientation, however, to help you see where your school sits on the faith "map" and understand something of the terms that you may hear used in the school. Thankfully, these days, although there are differences and divisions within the Christian faith, most Christians understand that the most important thing is to follow the example of Jesus and to put into practice his teachings – namely, to love our neighbour unconditionally.

TIP

You may or may not be familiar with the language of the Christian faith, so please don't feel put off if you don't understand some of the words and terms that are used in this book. Bear in mind that scholars and theologians have puzzled over the meanings of some of these terms for hundreds of years. At the back of the book you can find some simple definitions, along with a list of some of the excellent books and websites which are available to help you explore further. If you're not familiar with navigating your way around the Bible, there's a guide on page 8. In addition, a member of the clergy or a work colleague should be willing and able to talk through things with you – so don't be afraid to ask and keep asking. Remember that keeping an enquiring mind is a key part of any faith journey.

CHAPTER 2

> The highest education is that which brings the student face to face, not simply with something great but with someone great, namely Christ.
>
> *Donald Coggan (1909 – 2000), Archbishop of Canterbury*

Jesus Christ – at the heart of it all

As its name suggests, Christianity is built around Jesus Christ. Whatever their differences, all Christians have in common the fact that they have an important relationship with Jesus, who is at the heart of their faith. By far the best way to get to know this extraordinary man is through reading about him, about his life, works and wisdom. The best place to start with that is in the four Gospels.[1]

Christians believe that Jesus, the Son of God, came to live on earth among people as a demonstration of God's limitless love for, and commitment to, humanity. This idea – that God came to earth in human form, is known as the "incarnation", and is the main reason why Christians celebrate Christmas. There are hundreds of different ideas about this, and the truth is that this story of salvation is still being worked out. However, it's worth noting that Jesus was born into a Jewish family, in the Middle East, in very humble circumstances. So if you ever feel that Christianity is confined to well-off, middle-class people in the West, bear in mind Jesus' origins.

Jesus himself is a powerful and compelling character – someone many young people respond warmly to. Contrary to the expectations of the community he was born into, the Son of God did not demand honour, power and wealth for himself. He did not lord it over other people, or set out to create a grand institution. Indeed, he did not write anything down or draw up a list of rules. Rather, he put his time, energy and resources into teaching about the kingdom of God (in stories known as parables), serving and healing people – physically and emotionally as well as spiritually.

In particular, Jesus had boundless compassion and love for those who were marginalised or outcast in the society he lived in. Time and again he stood up to the authorities to champion the cause of poor people (Luke 16:19-31), women (Matthew 9:20-22), and those who were disabled (John 5:2-9) or culturally and socially disadvantaged (Luke 10:25-37). Through his teaching and actions, Jesus turned the thinking of the world on its head. In fact he was so radical, so extraordinary, that the truth is that Christians have struggled ever since to come to terms with what he represents.

Throughout his ministry, Jesus repeatedly told his followers (known as disciples) that he would die (Mark 8:31-33), but they did not fully understand him. The last time he ate with them (Mark 14:22-25) he even symbolically enacted the breaking up of his body (as bread) and the spilling of his blood (as wine) – a powerful gesture which Christians remember and re-enact when they share bread and wine at a form of worship known as Holy Communion (sometimes also called the Eucharist, or Mass) (see the glossary at the back of the book).

Jesus was right in predicting his own death. The authorities were enraged and frightened by his power and influence, and he was put on trial and sentenced to death by being crucified upon a cross. When he died, in around AD 30, he was only about thirty-three years old. Normally, of course, that would have been the end of it. But for Christians that's where the story really begins. Central to the Christian faith is the belief that Jesus was resurrected three days after his death. The resurrection represents many things for Christians – triumph over defeat, an end to death, the fulfilment of God's promise. After that he was taken up to heaven to be with God, his Father.

> **A NOTE ABOUT CHURCHES AND THE CHURCH**
>
> These terms are sometimes confusing. When we talk about the Christian Church, we are referring to the whole of Christianity. Within that, there are different Christian traditions that use the term "church" in their names (such as the Church of England or the Church in Wales) and, of course, church buildings.

Sowerby Village CE (VC) Primary School

The Christian Church

Before his death, Jesus nominated one of his disciples, Peter, to found the Christian Church (Matthew 16:18). Some of the books of the New Testament (particularly the book of Acts) relate how Peter and other followers of Jesus started to turn this into a reality.

Of course, the Christian Church is, like any organisation, made up of human beings, and over the years it has had its ups and downs, differences and divisions. On a few occasions these have caused major schisms, which are worth outlining as they have created the landscape of Christianity as we know it today. First, in the early eleventh century, the Church divided into the Eastern Church (sometimes known as Orthodox Christianity) and the Roman Catholic Church. More turbulence in the sixteenth century (now known as the Reformation) led to a further division and the rise of Protestantism.

CHAPTER 2

The Anglican Communion, the Church of England and the Church in Wales

Anglicanism is a form of Protestantism. The Anglican Communion, as it is known, is not a single Church, but is more accurately described as a Christian faith community. It is a huge community, with 85 million Anglican Christians in over 165 countries.[2] In effect it is a collection of traditions that share aspects of their history, tradition and ways of worshipping. No two churches are exactly alike, and this "unity in diversity" is one of the things that make the Anglican Communion so special.[3]

So how does all this affect the school I work in?

Above all, what you should find in a church school is a community underpinned by the deep belief that everyone is created by God and filled with the love of God. It might be difficult to see things that way on a dreary Monday morning, when Year 9 refuse to engage with one of Shakespeare's plays, or Year 5 have had enough of your numeracy strategy, or the canteen has been left in a complete state – again. But that is the truth of the matter. Our young people are not first and foremost "learners" or "citizens", and certainly not economic units. What you should see in any church school is this belief in practice, in every single policy and relationship. Christians believe that they are created by God to fulfil a God-given destiny, and that is why a church school should be a place of joy and celebration. In Christian terms, we are loved, we are saved, and life is good! The challenge is to embrace this gift.

What about other schools?

You may wonder about schools which don't have a faith identity and don't talk about any of these things. Do they not regard children as special and have caring staff committed to their well-being? Are they not places of joy? Of course they are, and they are every bit as committed to the education of their students. The difference is the foundation. Some commentators argue that schools funded by the state should be neutral and not favour one religion or ethos over another, but the fact is that every school has a way of looking at the person and society which informs every policy and decision. In the church school the difference is that this ideology is out in the open. In many other schools it's there, but implicit.

Some argue that church schools are divisive and seek to indoctrinate young people. In those terms all schools more or less indoctrinate children, or educate them according to a world view. Even if that view is "live and let live", it's still a view. The church school has a foundation in the Christian faith. By the nature of that foundation, the school should strive not only for the good of its students, but for the common good of society. Many who work in church schools feel a sense of personal calling to be part of such an enterprise.

Where am I in all this?

Do you have to believe all of the above in order to work in a church school? And what about all the rest of it – the beliefs, the morality, the Bible and so forth? The answer is that you certainly don't have to be a fully paid-up subscriber. In fact, there will be many

21

people working in church schools who don't know much about Christianity, and as we said earlier, you're not expected to be an expert. You may be sitting there in a school service or assembly thinking, "I'm really not sure I get this, or even believe it" – and you would not be alone. We are all on a journey and we are all at very different stages on that journey.

Those who work in a church school should certainly respect and support what the school is all about (you may be asked about that at your interview). Appointments are at the discretion of the governors, who may choose to employ practising Christians in some key teaching and non-teaching posts, such as the headteacher and, where appropriate, the head of religious studies and the chaplain. But for most of the staff who work in church schools there is no requirement to tick every box. You should of course be committed to developing personally and professionally to be as good as you can be in your role in the school, but above all there is an expectation that you are willing to be with the young people on their journey.

Mick Rhodes and his team

INTERVIEW – THE SCHOOL SITE MANAGER

I'm not practising, but I am a believer. I have been working in the school for twenty-seven years, and I've witnessed how being a faith-based school can really make a difference. It becomes part of you without you knowing it's part of you. As a form tutor the school's core values – Empathy, Honesty, Respect and Responsibility – definitely help, as I can always bring any discussion back to those.

As the site manager much of the work that I and my team do involves making the school available for different functions, such as assemblies. I am often asked to set up all kinds of things for worship. For example, my team and I have set up a steel band in Halifax Minster – that kind of thing isn't uncommon. It's hard work and you sometimes wonder why you're bothering, but then, when you see it all come together in a service, you realise.

I would advise anyone working in a church school who's not a believer not to be put off or frightened by the church stuff. It's not rammed down your throat. In fact I think it's educated me.

Mick Rhodes, Site Manager, Trinity Academy, Halifax

CHAPTER 2

POINTS TO REMEMBER

- There are shades of opinion in the Christian Church, just as everywhere, but beneath it there's a core message – and that's a message of love.
- You're on a journey – and right now you're here because you've been chosen.

POINTS FOR PERSONAL REFLECTION OR GROUP DISCUSSION

- Can you understand why around thirty million people in England and Wales identify as Christians?
- What did you know about the Christian faith before you took the job, and what was your main source of knowledge? Has that changed?
- Did you have any experience – positive or negative – of Christianity? If you have questions about it, where might you go for answers?

1. The term "Gospels" refers to the books of Matthew, Mark, Luke and John – the first four books of the New Testament in the Bible.
2. In some places (such as Scotland and the USA) Anglicans are known as Episcopalians.
3. You can find out more at: www.anglicancommunion.org

REFLECTION

The Lord God said: I myself will dream a dream within you;
Good dreaming comes from me, you know.
My dreams seem impossible,
Not too practical
Not for the cautious man or woman;
A little risky sometimes,
A trifle brash perhaps...
Some of my friends prefer
To rest more comfortably in sounder sleep with visionless eyes...
But from those who share my dreams
I ask a little patience, a little humour,
Some small courage, and a listening heart
– I will do the rest...
Then they will risk and wonder at their daring;
Run – and marvel at their speed...
Build – and stand in awe at the beauty of their building.
You will meet me often as you work in your companions who share the risk,
In your friends who believe in you enough
To lend their own dreams,
Their own hands,
Their own hearts, to your building.
In the people who will stand in your doorway,
Stay awhile, and walk away knowing that they too
Can find a dream...
There will be sin-filled days
And sometimes a little rain.
A little variety! Both come from me.
So come now – be content.
It is my dream you dream,
My house you build,
My caring you witness;
My love you share
And this is the heart of the matter.

"The Dream of God",
by Charles Péguy (1873 – 1914)

CHAPTER 3

The Background and History of Church Education in England and Wales

Schools for the community

It's important to understand that Church of England (C of E) and Church in Wales (C in W) schools exist for, and are run primarily for, the communities in which they are located. In other words, they're not there to recruit people for the Church, or to convert anyone, nor do they exist solely for the benefit of the Christian families in any particular area – they're there to serve all the people of their locality.

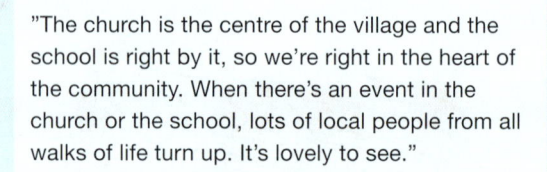

> "The church is the centre of the village and the school is right by it, so we're right in the heart of the community. When there's an event in the church or the school, lots of local people from all walks of life turn up. It's lovely to see."
>
> *Pat Crawshaw, Site Manager, Sowerby Village CE (VC) Primary School*

As the Church of England website puts it, church schools "are inclusive and serve equally those who are of the Christian faith, those of other faiths and those with no faith",[1] while the Church in Wales website states: "Our schools are inclusive by nature, serving children and young people in a range of communities. They also form a natural point of community focus, whether in the inner city or in rural villages."[2]

This emphasis on serving communities is no new idea but, as we shall see in this chapter, something which is deeply embedded in the foundations, history and ethos of church school education in England and Wales.

CHAPTER 3

A history lesson – how church schools began

The first church school in Great Britain is reckoned to be King's School in Canterbury, founded by Augustine of Canterbury (a missionary to England and the first Archbishop of Canterbury) in AD 597. Throughout the fifteenth, sixteenth and seventeenth centuries, choir schools were founded to educate choristers and "deserving poor" children. Alongside that was what could be termed the "charity school movement", with Christ's Hospital, the first Bluecoats school (named after its distinctive uniform), founded in 1552.

Griffith Jones and the Welsh Circulating Schools

Griffith Jones was born around 1683 at Penboyr in Carmarthenshire. He was ordained in 1708 and appointed rector of Llanddowror in 1716, where he remained for the rest of his life. In 1731 he established the first Circulating School, in order to teach people to read. The name came from the fact that the schools were established and run for a brief time by teachers who would then move on, having trained local teachers. Lessons were in Welsh, and the emphasis was on teaching basic literacy using religious texts provided by the Society for Promoting Christian Knowledge (SPCK – still a flourishing organisation and publishing house today). Teaching took place in a variety of buildings, including in one case a windmill.

Griffith Jones (1684 – 1761)

The National Society established schools in Wales and England, and by 1833, when the government began to contribute to the funding of education, there were 146 Anglican church schools in Wales, compared with only fifteen in England. It is estimated that over two hundred thousand people learnt to read in the Circulating Schools, and that by the time Griffith Jones died in 1761 there were three thousand five hundred such schools.

SOME KEY DATES IN WALES[3]

1699 – inaugural meeting of the Society for Promoting Christian Knowledge (SPCK).

1731 – Griffith Jones sets up the first Circulating School.

1811 – foundation of the National Society for the Education of the Poor in the Principles of the Established Church.

1833 – the National Society starts to receive an annual subsidy to establish schools. At this point there are 147 C in W schools in existence.

1870 – the Elementary Education Act establishes the framework for the schooling of all children between the ages of 5 and 13.

1916 – the disestablishment of the Anglican Church in Wales, meaning that Church and state become separated.

1944 – the Education Act makes schooling free for all pupils and raises the school leaving age to 15.

1965 – the largest expansion of comprehensive schools takes place.

1988 – the Education Reform Act establishes the National Curriculum and gives parents the right to choose which school their child should attend, or whether to home educate them instead.

Joshua Watson and the National Society

Much of what we know today is a result of the vision of Joshua Watson, the founder of the National Society.

Joshua Watson (1771 – 1855)

Joshua Watson was born in 1771 in Tower Hill, London. He was the second son of John Watson, who rose from humble beginnings to become a wealthy wine merchant and government contractor. Joshua's elder brother John went into the Church, becoming first Rector of St John's Church, Hackney, and then Archdeacon of St Albans. Joshua was sent to be an apprentice in book-keeping in preparation for entering his father's business. This motivated him to aspire to greater things, and by the age of forty-three he was sufficiently wealthy to retire from business in order to concentrate on other matters.

Joshua and his brother were part of a group known as the Hackney Phalanx. In 1811 they founded the National Society for the Education of the Poor in the Principles of the Established Church. At a time when education for all was held to be politically dangerous, this was a radical move. The aim of the National Society was to raise money by voluntary subscription to support the provision of a church school in every parish in England. Its stated purpose was that:

> "National Religion should be made the foundation of National Education, and should be the first and chief thing taught to the Poor, according to the excellent Liturgy and Catechism provided by our Church."[4]

With regard to children, the National Society's objectives were:

> "… to teach them the doctrine of Religion according to the principles of the Established Church, and to train them to the performance of their religious duties by an early discipline [and] to communicate such knowledge and habits as are sufficient though life in their proper station."[5]

The reference to "their proper station" might sound odd these days, but in the early nineteenth century this was a radical proposition. The National Society's educational objective was primarily religious instruction, but also general education in literacy and numeracy, to enable children from poor families to achieve their potential and escape the routine of child labour that was all too familiar in the mid-nineteenth century.[6]

The Sunday School movement

The driving forward of the Sunday School movement by Robert Raikes (1735 – 1811) further reinforced the Church's role in making education for school-aged children universally available regardless of class or income. As well as teaching scripture, Sunday Schools taught basic literacy to make the Bible and the Book of Common Prayer widely accessible, as well as to balance sacred and secular learning.

CHAPTER 3

Underlying the Sunday School movement and the foundation of the National Society was the increasing realisation during the nineteenth century that child labour – in mines, mills and factories – was a moral scandal which deprived children of even a basic education.

Church and state in education

A major step forward in the educational partnership between Church and state took place in 1833, when the Whig (Liberal) government voted to award the National Society an annual subsidy to help in the establishment of schools. From then on the provision of education for all, regardless of income or class, grew. This was consolidated in the 1944 Education Act.

During the 1950s, 1960s and 1970s, the debate around religious education shifted, as waves of migration to the UK created a far more multicultural, ethnically diverse society. Inevitably, questions started being asked about whether children in schools should learn about other faiths as well as Christianity. It is a debate that continues to this day. Perhaps because of this, and because of the introduction of the comprehensive school system, which sought to standardise education, it's fair to say that these decades were characterised by a shift away from faith-based education. That trend started to be reversed in the late 1980s, when the emphasis moved away from "one-size-fits-all" education, and greater parental choice was introduced. In 2001 a government Green Paper, *Schools: Building on Success*, recognised the value of faith-based schools and suggested a procedure for enabling community schools to become church schools through partnership with local education authorities.[7]

SOME KEY DATES IN ENGLAND

597 – foundation of the King's School, Canterbury – reputed to be the oldest school in England.

1699 – inaugural meeting of the Society for Promoting Christian Knowledge (SPCK).

1703 – Old Schools Trust (now the Church Schools of Cambridge) founded by the Revd William Whiston "to train poor children in the knowledge of God, and in the Christian Religion".[8]

1780 – the Sunday School movement, pioneered by Robert Raikes, is established as a national movement.

1811 – foundation of the National Society for the Education of the Poor in the Principles of the Established Church.

1830 – the Sunday School Union is formed – over 7,000 Sunday schools with 9,000 teachers and 845,000 pupils.[9]

1833 – the National Society starts to receive an annual subsidy to establish schools.

1870 – the Elementary Education Act establishes the framework for the schooling of all children between the ages of 5 and 13.

1944 – the Education Act makes schooling free for all pupils and raises the school leaving age to 15.

1965 – the largest expansion of comprehensive schools takes place.

1988 – the Education Reform Act establishes the National Curriculum and gives parents the right to choose which school their child should attend, or whether to home educate them instead.

> "I'm from a Catholic family and was brought up a Catholic, and my career up until now has been in Catholic schools. Actually, I really enjoy learning about my faith in this context, because the values link through different religions. For me, although I am still a committed Catholic, I'm finding that working in a Church of England school is expanding my horizons."
>
> *Katie Lopuszniak, Teacher in QT, Sowerby Village CE (VC) Primary School*

Church education in England and Wales today

Church schools in state education

Today over five hundred independent schools declare themselves in their trust deeds, mission statements or other documents to be Anglican in ethos,[10] while in the state sector the C of E and the C in W are important providers of education in partnership with local authorities.

A FEW STATISTICS[11]

- Approximately 1 million children and young people attend C of E schools and 25,000 attend C in W schools.
- About 15 million people alive today went to a C of E school.
- There are 4,500 C of E primary schools and over 200 C of E secondary schools.
- There are 172 C in W primary and secondary schools, supporting the careers of over 5,000 teachers and support staff.
- With more than 130 sponsored and 350 converter academies,[12] the Church is the biggest sponsor of academies in England (there are no academies in Wales).
- In the C of E alone, clergy dedicate an estimated 1 million hours every year to working with children and young people in schools, often providing holiday and after-school activities.

C of E and C in W schools have a long and highly respected heritage. The supporting bodies – the National Society, the Church of England Education Office and the Diocesan Boards of Education – play a key part in ensuring that children are educated to the highest standards, that appropriate staff are appointed and that leadership teams are fully robust and answerable to parents, staff and wider bodies.

CHAPTER 3

C OF E SCHOOLS HAVE AN EXCELLENT TRACK RECORD:

- 84% of C of E primary schools are rated "Good" or "Outstanding" by Ofsted, compared with 81% of non-C of E schools.

- 75% of C of E secondary schools are rated "Good" or "Outstanding" by Ofsted, compared with 71% of non-C of E schools.

- 92% of C of E primary schools and 90% of C of E secondary schools are rated "Good" or "Outstanding" under the SIAMS[13] inspection framework, which assesses levels of spiritual and pastoral support.[14]

The Bishop of St Asaph, the Rt Revd Gregory Cameron, opening the Nurture Room in Gungrog C in W Nursery and Infant School. Photo by Simon Cameron

As we have seen, church schools have a rich history in the provision of education for all in both England and Wales. This ethos of universal access to free education, which has inclusiveness at its heart, is still fundamental to the way in which C of E and C in W schools are run. As someone working in a church school, no matter what your role, you play a part in carrying forward the vision of Joshua Watson, albeit in a very different world from that of two hundred and fifty years ago. So it's a good idea to take some time to reflect on this and consider where you figure in this landscape, and how you can continue the tradition and carry it forward.

IN TERMS OF INCLUSIVENESS, C OF E SCHOOLS ARE BROADLY IN LINE WITH NATIONAL AVERAGES:

- 15% of C of E pupils are eligible for free school meals, in line with the national average.

- 25% of C of E pupils are from ethnic minority backgrounds, just 1% below the national average of 26%.[15]

POINTS TO REMEMBER

- C of E and C in W schools do not exist to recruit people for the Church, or to convert anyone, nor are they for the sole benefit of the Christian families in any particular area – they exist to serve all the people of their community.

- Since the beginning, the Church has played a major role in introducing education for all, with a particular concern to offer better opportunities to children from poor and disadvantaged backgrounds. This is very much part of the Church's ethos today.

POINTS FOR PERSONAL REFLECTION OR GROUP DISCUSSION

- Are you surprised to learn the extent to which the Church has always championed education for all, particularly for children from poor and disadvantaged backgrounds?

- How do you see the Church's ethos of education for all lived out in the school you work in?

- How might you as an individual further the vision and work of Joshua Watson, Griffith Jones and the National Society in your work?

PRAYER

In all our travelling
All: May your footsteps guide us
In our journeying to work and returning
All: May your footsteps guide us
Within our homes and families
All: May your footsteps guide us
In our leisure time together
All: May your footsteps guide us
In difficult situations and conflict
All: May your footsteps guide us
As we stumble on the way
All: May your footsteps guide us
In the travelling of our faith
All: May your footsteps guide us
As we place our trust in you
All: May your footsteps guide us

In all our travelling, Lord,
may it be your footsteps
in which we place our feet.

"Prayers Exploring our Daily Walk with Christ" © John Birch, www.faithandworship.com
Used by permission

---

1. The Church of England/Education & National Society/Church Schools and Academies: www.churchofengland.org
2. The Church in Wales/Schools/Education: www.churchinwales.org.uk
3. Powys Heritage Online: http://history.powys.gov.uk/history/common/educ6.html
4. *The Christian Remembrancer*, vol. I (F.C. & J. Rivington, 1819).
5. Quoted in David Blundell, *Education and Construction of Childhood* (London: Continuum, 2012).
6. Tim Elbourne, *Understanding Church Schools: Ideas for Today from Joshua Watson's Founding Vision* (Cambridge: Grove Booklets, 2012).
7. Department for Education and Employment, *Schools: Building on Success* (Norwich: HMSO, 2001).
8. The Church Schools of Cambridge: www.csoc.org.uk/history
9. H. Burgess, *Enterprise in Education* (London: SPCK, 1958), 13.
10. The Woodard Foundation: www.woodard.co.uk
11. Figures from the Church of England/Education: www.churchofengland.org; & the Church in Wales/Life/Schools: www.churchinwales.org.uk
12. Schools that were previously maintained and have voluntarily converted to academy status.
13. Statutory Inspection of Anglican and Methodist Schools.
14. Ofsted Summary of Latest Judgements, accurate as of 31 March 2014: www.churchofengland.org/education.aspx
15. Department for Education, 2013 School Census: www.churchofengland.org/education.aspx

Trinity Academy

CHAPTER 4

What is a Church School and How is it Different?

Working in a church school is very different from working in a school which is not based on Christianity – as indeed it ought to be. But of course all schools have a great deal in common when it comes to day-to-day aspects of running and working in them. Like any school, a church school has its challenges – the demands of the teaching curriculum jostle alongside the need to keep to timetables, provide nutritious food at mealtimes, juggle classrooms, stick to budgets, take health and safety into account, and provide sport and extracurricular activities. And of course so many young people growing up together makes a church school, like any other, a challenging and hopefully rewarding place to work.

You may well know all this already. But the point is that just because a church school is built upon a Christian foundation, it doesn't make the day-to-day logistics any easier to manage, it doesn't make it a rarefied place, and it doesn't necessarily make the people who work in it any holier than anyone else.

So what is different about a church school?

A church school should have a clear purpose and be informed by beliefs and values which are rooted in the Christian faith and guided by the example of Jesus. These should permeate every aspect of day-to-day learning and life in the school. They should not be based on coercion, or on rules for their own sake, but should spring from the school's ethos of justice, forgiveness, love and compassion.

If we want to identify the distinguishing features that make a church school different, we need to ask why it exists. The Church in Wales website begins its mission statement for schools with the words: "A Church School is a witness to the mission of Christ in the Gospel." That is an excellent starting point. And, more than that, Anglican Communion Churches have a particular focus on serving the community, not just their members. So let's take a closer look at what that means in practice.

EMPATHY   HONESTY   RESPECT   RESPONSIBILITY

CHAPTER 4

Church schools exist:
- because each child has his or her own unique character and God-given potential.
- to teach young people to acquire critical-thinking skills, write and speak articulately and discover their particular talents and vocation.
- to inspire their students to find out who they are, to learn about God, and to discover the reason for their existence on earth.
- to motivate their students to become people of *challenge, change and transformation:*

  - *challenge* – to see the world as God created it to be and to be unafraid and unashamed to challenge anything which stands in the way of that, or which denigrates or belittles the person. To see every person as a brother or sister made in the image and likeness of God. And, with this at the heart of their learning, not to tolerate anything less.

  - *change* – to be agents of and advocates for change where it is needed. To understand how to bring about change wisely, bravely and peacefully. Not to be afraid to persevere when the going gets tough.

  - *transformation* – to be personally transformed and, through this transformation, to be able to see the world from God's perspective and work towards a vision of a transformed world. To be ablaze with a passion for justice and peace.

The Gospel message and the example of Jesus underpin each of these points – and *that* is the key difference between a church school and any other. You will think that they are very high ideals – and indeed they are – but that is what church schools are founded for.

In line with these ideals and this uncompromising spirit, a church school should be a "big picture" place – a living community where everyone is educated in heart and soul as well as mind. Following Jesus' example, it should be a place where everyone is equally respected and unconditionally loved – a community which wants to reach out to all, especially those who are poor and marginalised, and those in greatest need. While there are many very good schools, staffed by very good people (many of whom, of course, will be informed in their work by their faith), Christian educationalists believe that education is infinitely richer for having these clear ideals at its heart. To put it simply – a church school is where life, faith and culture are one.

Christians believe that God so loved the world that, in spite of the fact that people were making such a mess of everything, God would not abandon humankind. Rather, God sent Jesus as a human being, to be born, live, die and rise again, to show us once and for all just who we are and how much we are loved, and to give us the example of a perfect life.

Following the example of Jesus, the Church should go first to those in the greatest need and support a church school there. It is not a matter of opening a church school and forcing people to be Christians, to believe anything or to live a certain kind of lifestyle. The role of the church school is to educate in the broadest sense of the word, because education empowers and liberates. What each person does with the knowledge and experiences they receive through working or studying at a church school is up to them.

INTERVIEW – THE PRINCIPAL'S PA

I'm a Christian, and in everything I do I try to represent what Christianity is. For me personally, the Ten Commandments cover absolutely everything in daily life, and in our school they are simplified in our four core values – Empathy, Honesty, Respect and Responsibility. That doesn't mean they're watered down in any way, but more accessible for everyone and I feel they genuinely underpin everything that we do in the school.

I like to say that "Doing the right thing isn't always easy, but it is always right." I often find myself dealing with difficult situations in my role and it is always a balance between the academic needs of the students, the business needs of the school and considerations for staff welfare and happiness. When I find myself in these situations I spend time, no so much praying, but reflecting upon my faith, past experiences and knowledge to ensure I deal with any situation in, not the easiest, but the RIGHT way. As my colleagues and the students share the same values, it is easy to use them as touchstones to help frame a discussion, however difficult.

We serve a disadvantaged area and many of our students have to deal with very difficult home situations on a daily basis. We are not only committed to providing an educational experience that enables students to fulfil their academic potential, but also supporting their personal needs, social development and enhancing their moral values and cultural experiences. We feel privileged to work with our students to instil self-belief and show them that they can do anything if they put their mind to it.

Dianne Alcock, Principal's PA,
Trinity Academy, Halifax

CHAPTER 4

> **THE DEFINITION OF EDUCATION**
>
> The word "education" has two Latin root words. One is *"educere"*, meaning "to lead forth", or "to lead out of". The other root word is *"educare"*, meaning "to support and nurture".

How is working in a church school different?

As we saw at the beginning of this chapter, many of the day-to-day aspects of your work will not be substantially different from working in any other school. A key difference when you work in a church school is that you – whatever your own faith, background or views – are invited and encouraged to contribute to the school's ethos, because that is its foundation and should inform everything. If you are not a Christian, this may come as a surprise. But don't be tempted to compartmentalise your contribution or get into the mindset of: "I'm just here to work – I leave the religious bit to other people." Remember that everyone in any school is in some way a teacher. In light of the Church's views on the vital importance of education, and by virtue of the fact that the headteacher and school governors have given you the job, you are deemed to be someone who can contribute to the school and community in every respect, including its faith life.

So what does that mean? Well, it has nothing to do with converting to Christianity or forcing yourself to believe anything. It has everything to do with being fully engaged with your work and your work environment, and knowing that you have a significant contribution to make.

Is there anyone who should not work in a church school?

Yes – the cynic with a closed mind, who refuses to engage with questions of faith. It would be unwise for anyone to apply to a church school if they felt unable to support what the school is all about, because they would feel unhappy and ill at ease in their work. It would be a stressful and draining experience and, in turn, the pupils would pick this up and it would undermine the school's aims and mission.

If you accept a post in a C in W or C of E school, you should be comfortable with the whole package – the way of life, thinking and being. That's not to say that you're not allowed to question or challenge anything, or express any doubts, but it is important to spend time reflecting on the important questions of spirituality and ethos, and the part they play in your life.

The National Curriculum

In England, Wales and Northern Ireland, all teaching is set within the context of the National Curriculum. The National Curriculum was introduced in all state schools in England, Wales and Northern Ireland in 1988, to ensure that each pupil is given the same standard of education. The National Curriculum broadly follows the same pattern and covers a similar range of subjects in all UK schools. Faith schools have to follow the National Curriculum, although academies have a little more freedom. Independent and private schools are less restricted in respect of the teaching curriculum. Religious studies (RS) is an important part of a balanced curriculum in any school. The key difference in a church school is that *all* learning is set within a Christian context.

Spiritual, moral, social and cultural (SMSC) education – the first entitlement of every child

Spiritual, moral, social and cultural (SMSC) education is the term that educators use to describe the broader dimension of education. Although it is a priority for all schools, it is worth looking at it in this context, as the values and priorities it emphasises are fundamentally in step with church education.

The 1988 Education Reform Act put spirituality on the teaching agenda for all schools in England, Wales and Northern Ireland. It states that every child is entitled to be taught a curriculum which:

(a) promotes the spiritual, moral, cultural, mental and physical development of pupils at the school; and

(b) prepares pupils for the opportunities, responsibilities and experiences of adult life.[1]

It means that, regardless of faith background, every school must educate its children and young people spiritually, morally, socially and culturally, and Ofsted inspectors must consider pupils' spiritual, moral, social and cultural development when forming a judgement of a school. In addition, as of November 2014, schools must promote British values.

Far from being confined to religious studies, SMSC education encompasses all aspects of learning, including extracurricular and out-of-school activities. It has four main components:

Spiritual education

According to the *School Inspection Handbook*, published by Ofsted[2] in 2015, the spiritual development of pupils is shown by their:

- ability to be reflective about their own beliefs, religious or otherwise, that inform their perspective on life and their interest in and respect for different people's faiths, feelings and values.

- sense of enjoyment and fascination in learning about themselves, others and the world around them.

- use of imagination and creativity in their learning.

- willingness to reflect on their experiences.

In church school terms, we might add that this concerns what people believe about the big questions of the meaning and purpose of life. It is everything about our existence on this planet that is beyond the material.

Moral education

Ofsted says that the moral development of pupils is shown by their:

- ability to recognise the difference between right and wrong and to readily apply this understanding in their own lives, recognise legal boundaries and, in so doing, respect the civil and criminal law of England.

- understanding of the consequences of their behaviour and actions.

- interest in investigating and offering reasoned views about moral and ethical issues and ability to understand and appreciate the viewpoints of others on these issues.

Because of what someone believes about the purpose and meaning of life, they live by principles and codes which guide their sense of right and wrong and the choices they make.

Social education

In Ofsted's definition, the social development of pupils is shown by their:

- use of a range of social skills in different contexts – for example, working and socialising with other pupils, including those from different religious, ethnic and socio-economic backgrounds.

- willingness to participate in a variety of communities and social settings, including by volunteering, cooperating well with others and being able to resolve conflicts effectively.

- acceptance of and engagement with the fundamental British values of democracy, the rule of law, individual liberty and mutual respect and tolerance of those with different faiths and beliefs; they develop and demonstrate skills and attitudes that will allow them to participate fully in and contribute positively to life in modern Britain.

This is about how people relate to the self and others, as well as the society they live in, which is influenced by spirituality and their moral code.

Cultural education

According to Ofsted, the cultural development of pupils is shown by their:

- understanding and appreciation of the wide range of cultural influences that have shaped their own heritage and others'.
- understanding and appreciation of the range of different cultures within school and further afield as an essential element of their preparation for life in modern Britain.
- knowledge of Britain's democratic parliamentary system and its central role in shaping our history and values, and in continuing to develop Britain.
- willingness to participate in and respond positively to artistic, musical, sporting and cultural opportunities.
- interest in exploring, improving understanding of and showing respect for different faiths and cultural diversity and the extent to which they understand, accept, respect and celebrate diversity, as shown by their tolerance and attitudes towards different religious, ethnic and socio-economic groups in the local, national and global communities.[3]

This concerns the ways in which people do things – the rites, rituals, customs and practices which develop over time within communities. Culture gives expression to a community's spirituality, morality and social values.

So how does a church school respond to SMSC education?

The fact that so much importance is attached to SMSC education is indicative of the extent to which the government recognises the significance of the role that schooling plays in a young person's life and understands that education is far more than a prescribed teaching curriculum. That, of course, is something that church schools have always understood and it has informed policy and procedure in C of E and C in W schools for many years, so it has been relatively straightforward for church schools to adopt the principles of SMSC education. Teachers should be aware of how SMSC values are being delivered through their lessons and subject area.

Spiritual education is not always so easy for schools that do not have a faith foundation, as it can be difficult to define what spiritual education is and its relationship with moral, social and cultural values. Without a religious framework such as the Bible and example of Christ to draw upon, it can be tricky to find and agree on a core set of beliefs and values that inform policy and procedure in the school.

You might ask: "Isn't a church school guilty of forcing God into everything?" – but the important thing is not to force God on people, but to honour God in everything. One school's vision, for example, is to provide the best quality education for the students in its catchment area. That in itself is honouring God, without forcing any particular outlook or belief onto anyone.

Does academic attainment come second in a church school?

Absolutely not! Far from diluting academic teaching, the Christian ethos and sense of purpose should make teaching truly three-dimensional, filling it with a heightened sense of wonder and curiosity, and imbuing it with a sense of meaning and purpose.

As we saw in Chapter Three, church schools consistently outperform national averages. In educating the whole person, a church school strives to ensure excellence for all. But as well as academic excellence, learning is situated within the context of Christian beliefs and values, because all learning is seen as interconnected. One area informs another and helps to make sense of some of the questions raised. A good church school makes those connections so that the pupils can learn about and from a subject, but also see *why* they are studying it.

So how do the Christian agenda and the National Curriculum sit side by side?

In a church school, Christian beliefs and values should provide the context for, and substantially shape, how the National Curriculum is applied and taught. Critical thinking is at the heart of any good learning – and this view is deeply held among Christian educators. It leads to deep learning, which is the opposite of rote learning, and encourages questioning, personal growth and wisdom. Across the taught curriculum, teachers in church schools strive to ensure that the big questions concerning the purpose and meaning of life are raised and faced. Often there are no simple answers, but the important thing is to engage with and explore these issues with questioning minds and honest hearts. In this way the teacher ends up with a radical, exciting and challenging curriculum in which questioning, intellectual curiosity and critical thinking are encouraged.

It's important to emphasise that this does not mean that there are not very good schools, teachers and educators working in other types of school. But the difference, as we have seen in previous chapters, is that the beliefs and values of the Christian faith, spirituality and ethos underpin *everything* and should influence every aspect of a church school.

> "C of E schools are committed to putting the big questions of life, purpose and meaning at the heart of the curriculum and to equipping pupils to be able to form their own approaches to life, whether informed by Christian or religious commitment or not. C of E schools encourage pupils to express their personal beliefs and philosophies with confidence and in an atmosphere of open and critical discussion." [4]

INTERVIEW – THE MARKETING DIRECTOR

I am a Christian but someone who "dips in and out". I married in church, and had my daughter christened, but I don't go all that often and sometimes I question my own faith during difficult events.

I really believe we're making a generational difference in our catchment area. Some of our students' parents did not have the best experience of education themselves. North Halifax, where we are located, is in an area of significant deprivation. The Academy is making a huge difference to students, and I believe it is changing views of education by giving students fantastic opportunities, regardless of personal or financial circumstance. I think we've found a magic formula – it's a balance between pushing the students to academic success and giving them a solid grounding in the school's values – Empathy, Honesty, Respect and Responsibility. It's not a question of rote learning – they really do have a meaning for them, rooted in the school's Christian ethos.

Hayley Wilson, Marketing Director, Trinity Academy, Halifax

Christianity, the National Curriculum and the two great commandments

There was a time when prevalent Christian ideas meant that the Church was in some respects out of kilter with society and the secular education system. This was particularly relevant when it came to sexual morality and lifestyle. That is not to say that the debate has been resolved, and it is not the place of this book to enter into the discussion, save to say that in recent years greater emphasis has been placed on the two "great commandments", rather than getting hung up on the detail or being prescriptive about anybody's lifestyle choices.

This tension between the letter of the law and the spirit of the law is by no means a new phenomenon, and much of Jesus' teaching centred around bringing people back to the first principles of love, compassion, tolerance and inclusion. To gain a deeper understanding of this, our first port of call is the Bible, and in particular the Gospel of Matthew, chapter 22.

When he was preaching in Jerusalem towards the end of his three-year ministry, Jesus attracted a huge following of people for whom his words and wisdom must have been a breath of fresh air. This caused a great deal of discomfort for the Pharisees – men who belonged to a Jewish sect that was preoccupied with the detail of Jewish Law. Their interpretation of the Law was petty and pedantic and had nothing to do with the underlying principles. In other words, they were hung up on the letter of the law and ignored the spirit of the law.

In Matthew 22, we read how some of them pretended to be interested in Jesus' teaching, but in reality they were trying to catch him out and "plotted to entrap him in what he said" (Matthew 22:15). When they asked him: "Teacher, which commandment in the law is the greatest?", Jesus replied:

> "You shall love the Lord your God with all your heart, and with all your soul, and with all your mind." This is the greatest and first commandment. And a second is like it: "You shall love your neighbour as yourself." On these two commandments hang all the law and the prophets.
>
> *Matthew 22:37-40*

Just spend a bit of time thinking about those beautiful, liberating words and what they might mean for you.

Sometimes this passage is understood to mean that none of the detail of the law is important, although elsewhere in Matthew's Gospel Jesus strongly contradicted this view:

> Do not think that I have come to abolish the law or the prophets; I have come not to abolish but to fulfill. For truly I tell you, until heaven and earth pass away, not one letter, not one stroke of a letter, will pass from the law until all is accomplished.
>
> *Matthew 5:17-18*

God's laws are not irrelevant or something to be disregarded, but are to be engaged with fully, and followed with all our hearts and all our minds.

So how does this apply to life in a church school?
Like the Church, C in W and C of E schools are, of course, made up of individuals, each of whom has his or her individual response to Christianity, ethical matters and ideas about how children and young people should be educated. There will undoubtedly be differences of opinion, some of which will at times be irreconcilable. That is human nature. In addition, it's possible that church schools may feel obliged to adopt or respond to prevailing cultural norms and values in certain respects. And while Christian educationalists know and acknowledge that young people need to be prepared for the real world, the church school is driven by beliefs, values and a spirituality which takes it far beyond prevailing cultural trends or any government agenda. However, not only is it possible to meet these challenges head-on, it can also be rewarding and fulfilling.

Christians believe that it is through prayer and reflection that they come to understand this more deeply and to discern God's will for them.
The teaching from Matthew's Gospel is a wonderful story to bear in mind in the context of a school, where the rules are important, as is the governing framework within which the school operates.
What is more important, however, is to remember that each and every child and each and every member of staff should be valued and treated with respect as a son or daughter of God. Laws, rules, instructions, guidelines, procedures and policy should all, ultimately, point to loving God and one another.

POINTS TO REMEMBER

- Just because a church school is built upon a Christian foundation, it doesn't make the day-to-day logistics any easier to manage.
- The school's ethos and values should not be based on coercion, or on rules for their own sake, but should be founded on justice, forgiveness, love and compassion.
- The principles of spiritual, moral, social and cultural (SMSC) education apply to each and every school, and should be part of the fabric and culture of a church school.
- If you don't see the above points manifested in every aspect of the life and learning of the school, you are in just as much of a position to question and challenge it as anyone else.

PRAYER

Lord Jesus, who taught us to respect children;
Help us to face the challenge of educating the young people in our care with compassion, courage, grace and good cheer:
To make our school a place of distinction,
where you are honoured and your example,
is a shining light for all who work and study here,
for the Church and our community.
We pray this in your name.
Amen.

POINTS FOR PERSONAL REFLECTION OR GROUP DISCUSSION

- Has any part of this chapter challenged you? If so, why?
- Can you see yourself as a person of *challenge*, *change* and *transformation*?
- How do the principles of SMSC education relate to you, your life and your work?
- Would you agree that setting learning within the context of Christian beliefs and values brings it alive?
- Can you think of any ways in which Christian morality and ethics might be at odds with the secular society within which the Church is situated?
- Have you noticed a shift in ideas about morality and ethics in recent years? If so, do you think it is for the better?
- Do you think you could explain to someone else why the Church is so committed to education?

[1] *National Curriculum in England: Framework for Key Stages 1 to 4*: www.gov.uk/government/publications
[2] Ofsted inspects schools in England. In Wales, the inspecting body is Estyn.
[3] Ofsted, *School Inspection Handbook*: www.gov.uk/government/publications/school-inspection-handbook-from-september-2015
[4] Frequently Asked Questions about Church Schools: www.churchofengland.org

7x5=35
8x5=40
9x5=45
10x5=50
5x7=35
5x8=40
5x9=45
5x10=50
1x10=10
2x10=20
3x10=30
4x10=40
5x10=50
6x10=60
7x10=70
8x10=80
9x10=90
10x10=100
10x4=40
10x5=50
10x6=60
10x7=70
10x8=80
10x9=90
40÷4=10
50÷5=10
60÷6=10
70÷7=10
80÷8=10
90÷9=10
40÷10=4
50÷10=5
60÷10=6
70÷10=7
80÷10=8
90÷10=9
multiplied by
multiply
product
groups of
lots of
times
2M Going Home Arrangements

CHAPTER 5

Christian Spirituality and Ethos

In the last chapter we looked at what makes a church school different, and in this chapter we will take a closer look at one vitally important aspect of that difference.

Most people in our secular day and age go about their daily business without giving much thought to the "big questions" in life. Christians, however, believe we are infinitely richer if we do face those questions, and if in doing so we acknowledge that we *are* spiritual beings.

You may protest: "But I took this job because I need to pay my rent / put food on the table / support my family, and it's near to where I live – what's that got to do with being spiritual?"

Spirituality isn't confined to the clergy, saints or pious people. Whether we know it or not, we are *all* spiritual beings, longing for fulfilment and purpose in our lives. The difference, however, is that Christians believe that spirituality, based on the person of Jesus and his teachings, is the driving force, the expression of all that we are and do, think and feel. What's more, that's not just confined to an hour on a Sunday morning, but is something which permeates every aspect of our lives, including those things that are apparently mundane – even on the first day back at school after the summer break!

> "Last year one of our colleagues died. Although he had been ill, it was still a huge shock to everyone, as we're a very close community. The support the vicar gave us really helped. She came to counsel us as a group. She lit a candle and said prayers with us. More than that, though, she was available to us as individuals – through social media, on the phone – she was just there. I think a lot of us found that really comforting."
>
> *Vanessa Kitson, Catering Manager,*
> *Sowerby Village CE (VC) Primary School*

Engaging with the big questions sometimes means facing difficult realities that we would prefer to ignore – forgiveness, for example, or death. Just pause for a moment to think about how those two things have affected you. It's little wonder that people choose to live on the surface of life and opt for all kinds of distractions. But Christians believe that if we embrace spirituality, every aspect of life acquires new meaning and real purpose. Life might not be easier – but it will be richer, deeper, more fulfilling and worthwhile.

44

CHAPTER 5

You may ask: "But I'm just a cook / a classroom assistant / a caretaker / a physics teacher – what's that got to do with being spiritual?"

In a church school there is no such thing as a secular education, and spirituality is not confined to the classroom or formal education. Christians see every activity, every moment, as an opportunity to learn – and that includes mealtimes, break times, the journey to school, the journey home, and every waking and sleeping moment in between.

Whether you are a cook, a classroom assistant, a caretaker or a teacher, the idea of bringing spirituality into your work might seem daunting, but it means that your job ceases to be "just a job" and becomes a vocation, and you start to see that you are engaged in something much bigger. And it doesn't have to involve a huge personal change. We complicate our lives so much that becoming switched on to our spiritual side is actually, by contrast, blissfully simple. It's not about adding or achieving anything; it's about letting go and relaxing into being who we really are:

> Discovering vocation does not mean scrambling toward some prize just beyond my reach but accepting the treasure of true self I already possess. Vocation does not come from a voice out there calling me to be something I am not. It comes from a voice in here calling me to be the person I was born to be.
>
> *Thomas Merton*
> *Writer and mystic*

Brothers and sisters and children of God

In much the same way that Christians see every moment as precious and interconnected, so they believe that each individual is priceless and that all people are deeply connected. We are all part of God's family as brothers and sisters, and what happens to you happens to me. So you may hear expressions such as:

- Everyone belongs to the people of God.
- Together we make up the Body of Christ.
- We are all called to live in communion.

Often when we hear expressions like this we dismiss them as impossible – things that would be good in a perfect world. Sure, all Christians don't go around all the time feeling totally "at one" with each other – at times you'll see disharmony and discord in your school, just as you would in any other environment. But there is an underlying ideal and a heartfelt belief that we *are* all connected even if we don't act as though we are, and that with practice and faith we can experience this for ourselves.

> Are not five sparrows sold for two pennies? Yet not one of them is forgotten in God's sight. But even the hairs of your head are all counted. Do not be afraid; you are of more value than many sparrows.
>
> *Luke 12:6-7*

45

If we start to recognise the connection between ourselves and other people, we start to see others as God sees them – beautiful, amazing, full of possibilities and potential. In the context of a Christian education, then, the challenge is to help children and young people discover their full potential and recognise and value it in the people around them. Of course nobody appears beautiful or particularly good all the time – this is the ongoing challenge! But you are working in an environment where striving to meet this challenge is not just desirable, it is essential – a core reason for the very existence of the school and everyone within it.

> There is no longer Jew or Greek, there is no longer slave or free, there is no longer male and female; for all of you are one in Christ Jesus.
>
> *Galatians 3:28*

A long tradition of pastoral care

Pastoral care is central to the ethos and identity of a church school. St John Baptist De La Salle, one of several patron saints of teachers,[1] who lived and worked in education over three hundred years ago, stressed the need for teachers to "touch hearts", so that each student felt valued as unique and loved. This individual and important approach was to demonstrate that those who were in positions of care for young people carried out their roles with the development of the whole person as a high priority. Of course, any good school will have a caring and professional pastoral care system. The difference in a church school is that the foundation and inspiration for the care offered to students and staff comes from a commitment to the Gospel and the person of Jesus Christ. It may not feel like it on a wet Monday afternoon in January, but what is being offered to that Year 5 boy in distress, or that Year 9 girl in confusion, is no less than the love of God in human form. The pastoral system in the church school is there not just to pick up the pieces when things go wrong, but actively to promote the flourishing of the students.

> "Christian ethos and the distinctiveness of a church school should not be relegated to nor emerge from the chaplain and RS department. They should not be restricted to acts of worship or extra-curricular activities. The aim should be for these principles and values to be owned by governors, the senior leadership team and indeed the whole staff."[2]

Respect

"Very simply this is about always being nice, and treating others and objects in the right way."

Ben B

Trinity Academy Halifax

INTERVIEW – THE RESTAURANT MANAGER

I'm a practising Catholic and our children attend Methodist worship with the Brownies and Guides – so I see it from all angles. It's good to see different people from different faiths getting along so well.

The problems I do see arise from the fact that the school is in a really deprived community. I think I get particular insight into that from the kitchen and dining area. I and my team are some of the first staff to arrive and we see students turning up as early as 6.45 a.m. For some, it's because their parents need to go to work and they have nowhere else to go; for others it's because they feel safer here than they do at home. I've also seen some of them piling food high on their plates, because they don't know where their next meal is coming from. I've washed a school uniform now and again.

*Paula Barlow, Restaurant Manager,
Trinity Academy, Halifax*

CHAPTER 5

What is Christian spirituality?

Theologians discuss and debate what spirituality is – but a useful working definition is that spirituality is seeking to *know* God, rather than seeking to know *about* God. But it's also practical – in other words, our spirituality can be defined as the reason why we do what we do and the way in which we do it. We act in a particular way because of what we believe about the purpose and meaning of life. The greatest and most powerful aspect of a person is their spirit.

The Beatitudes

There is a set of Jesus' teachings which appear in the Gospels of Matthew and Luke. These, known as the Beatitudes, are a good starting point for thinking about spirituality. The word "Beatitude" comes from the Latin *"beatus"* which means "happy", "fortunate" or "blissful". In the Beatitudes, Jesus gives us a vision of what we might call "spirituality in action":

> Blessed are the poor in spirit, for theirs is the kingdom of heaven. Blessed are those who mourn, for they will be comforted. Blessed are the meek, for they will inherit the earth. Blessed are those who hunger and thirst for righteousness, for they will be filled. Blessed are the merciful, for they will receive mercy. Blessed are the pure in heart, for they will see God. Blessed are the peacemakers, for they will be called children of God. Blessed are those who are persecuted for righteousness' sake, for theirs is the kingdom of heaven.
>
> *Matthew 5:3-10*

In an age when people equated wealth, power and being busy with virtue, this was radical, subversive spirituality and a rousing call to live peacefully and humbly with one another – a vision of a life filled with compassion and love. Two thousand years later, Jesus' teachings have been so influential that they underpin our ideas about social justice and morality – not just for Christians, but in the wider cultural context. Most of us, whatever our faith or background, are profoundly influenced by this amazing man who stood on a mountain all those years ago and turned conventional thinking on its head.

CHAPTER 5

The Holy Trinity

Christian spirituality is rooted in the Holy Trinity – the source and centre of the Christian faith – and generally acknowledged to be a very difficult teaching to begin to comprehend! Indeed it is, and always will be, pure mystery. But at the same time it is absolutely fundamental to the faith – and many people who have spent time reflecting on it find it breathtaking, a mystery full of beauty.

The word "trinity" has its origins in the Latin for "three", and the study of the Holy Trinity is about the relationship between three "persons" (as they are known by the Church) – God the Father, Jesus the Son and the Holy Spirit. One helpful way to understand the Trinity comes from the Early Years Foundation Stage, where this very difficult concept is brilliantly explained by teachers. They make the sign of the cross and, as they touch their forehead, they say:

> Dear God, may all my thinking and learning (hand on forehead to symbolise God the Father)
>
> All my loving (hand on heart – Jesus the Son)
>
> And everything I do today (touching either shoulder – the Holy Spirit)
>
> be my best for you.

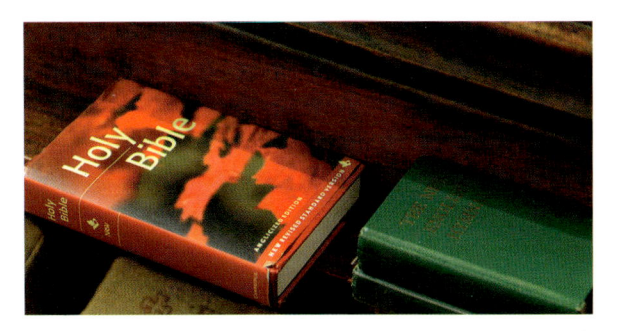

Sowerby Village CE (VC) Primary School

The school vision and mission statements

An individual school's spiritual ethos and outlook is defined in its vision and mission statement. Any organisation needs a vision, which is then put into practice through its mission. Taken together, these things give it cohesion and purpose.

Here are some examples of church schools' vision and mission statements:

> Our vision is to inspire each and every student to achieve their potential through high-quality teaching provided within an environment led by our Christian values. The four values of Empathy, Honesty, Respect and Responsibility are used in all our communication and form our mission.
>
> *Trinity Academy, Halifax*

> Wanting the best for each member of the school – within a Christian environment, gladly working in partnership with each other, with home, Church and the community – led by the hand of God.
>
> *Holy Trinity C of E Junior School, Wallington*

> Our successful Christian school offers a wide range of exciting and educational opportunities to enhance skills, talents and creativity. The school community appreciates and accepts others, and celebrates the achievements of all. We have supportive and trusting relationships with God and all his children. As a result, we take responsibility and welcome absolutely everyone into a caring and safe environment, where we are all guided to work together.
>
> *Moseley C of E Primary School*

Another good example of how Christian spirituality and ethos can inform the vision and mission in church education is provided by the mission statement of the Church in Wales:

THE MISSION STATEMENT OF THE CHURCH IN WALES

A church school is a witness to the mission of Christ in the Gospel:

- where Jesus Christ is our foundation;
- where every person has equal value and the chance to grow and develop to their full potential;
- where teachers, staff, governors and parents are committed to the education and development of the whole person;
- where the search for knowledge is accompanied by a quest for faith and a journey of spiritual experience;

so that…

- every child can learn of the richness of the created world, and grasp every opportunity to contribute to it in life;
- every member of staff can be nurtured in their vocation to teach;
- every achievement can be celebrated and every shortcoming forgiven;
- every person in this school can know that they are made in the image of God.

Every school should be a special place, a safe place, a place of learning, a place of nurture and of exploration. A school must demonstrate openness and acceptance, tolerance and forgiveness. Here, values and attitudes are formed and every individual is celebrated as unique.

A church school is all of these things and develops a distinctive Christian character through learning, religious studies, prayer, worship and action in the name of Christ that makes God's love and presence known to the world.

Note how far-reaching these statements are in intention, and how inclusive and loving their language is. It is clear that each of these schools is about far more than simply getting good academic results. Of course those things matter, but if a school reduces its mission to results at all costs, this should sound alarm bells and raise questions: "What is being neglected?", "Is the mission of the Church being carried out?", "Has another agenda crept in?"

Nor is it down to subscribing to a single belief system. Too often, church schools are thought to be places where people are indoctrinated or forced to think in a certain way. These statements show that the life of a church school is far richer than that.

> **TIP**
>
> Take a bit of time to reflect on or pray about these mission statements. Ask yourself how each point relates to you, the school that you work in and the wider community. In your reflection, do you feel that you need to change anything in yourself, or challenge anything in your workplace?

The importance of your contribution to the spirituality and ethos of the school

A church school is not just a collection of individuals, or a factory churning out students with good academic grades, but a community that bears witness to a common vision and mission. The young people who come to the school to learn come not as empty vessels to be filled with knowledge but, through their relationship with you and each other, to discover what it is to be human and the place that God has in their lives.

It should be clear to you by now that this means, not that you have to "buy into" every statement of belief, but that you need to recognise and appreciate the ethos of the school and value the school as a place which is underpinned by and imbued with a sense of Christian spirituality.

How do I find out more about Christianity?

The Bible

If you work in a teaching role, it's a really good idea to read up about Christianity and, as we've already seen, the Bible is the best place to start. It is definitely a good idea to own a Bible, and to turn to it when you want answers to questions – your own or someone else's. It may be bewildering at first, but soon you will start to find your way around it.[3] More than that, it's a good idea to sit quietly with it – if possible every day – and familiarise yourself with this extraordinary book – the most read book ever. For many people, Christian and non-Christian, the Bible is a source of wisdom, understanding, history, morality and spiritual strength – your single most valuable resource.

> So then, brothers and sisters, stand firm and hold fast to the traditions that you were taught by us, either by word of mouth or by our letter.
>
> *2 Thessalonians 2:15*

CHAPTER 5

POINTS TO REMEMBER

- Keep it simple. You don't need a theology degree to engage with these vast questions, or with matters of spirituality and ethos. You are already a fully spiritual being, and you have an ethos. What is important is that you do engage with that.

- You are on a journey and it will last a lifetime!

- Identify someone in your school you feel you can go to, to clarify anything you don't understand.

- Begin where you are and never mind where anyone else seems to be.

POINTS FOR PERSONAL REFLECTION OR GROUP DISCUSSION

- Has this chapter enabled you to reflect on your own spirituality? Have you seen anything in a new or different way?

- How comfortable or confident would you be talking about spiritual matters with colleagues and pupils?

- Take some time to read your school's mission statement. Are there any examples where you have seen it in action? Or where you have seen it disregarded? How does it apply to you in practical terms, and in how you do your job?

PRAYER

Disturb us, Lord, when
We are too well pleased with ourselves,
When our dreams have come true
Because we have dreamed too little,
When we arrive safely
Because we sail too close to the shore.
Disturb us, Lord, to dare more boldly,
To venture on wider seas
Where storms will show your mastery;
Where losing sight of land,
We shall find stars.

Sir Francis Drake

1. The other well-known patron saint of teachers is St Catherine of Alexandria.
2. Diane Tregale, *Fresh Experiences of School Chaplaincy* (Cambridge: Grove Books, 2011).
3. See page 8 for more about the Bible and how to read it.

INTERVIEW – THE SCHOOL CHAPLAIN

The school's core Christian values are embedded in the school's DNA, and everything is based on them. They inform the school's behaviour policy, its rewards policy, and every conversation or exchange that takes place in the school – everything.

Alongside our year groups we have a form structure. Every member of staff, whose schedule allows for it, is assigned to a form. Whether you are a teacher, the site manager or an administrator, you are also a form tutor. Each form is made up of about twenty students taken at random from the year groups, so it includes students of all ages.

Each day starts at 8.15 a.m. with the first lesson, followed by VT (vertical tutor) time. This is when the forms come together. There may be some academic content, but it's not subject-based and includes a reflection on an image – I come up with a new image each week – which is projected onto a wall in the middle of the school and displayed in the rooms where the forms are. The image will often be of something topical, which is a touchstone for reflecting upon the four core values. Together, the students and their form tutors discuss and reflect on the story behind the image.

Each day, VT time ends with two minutes of silent reflection, when the whole school stops and falls silent. You will literally see someone walking along a corridor, then just stop in their tracks when the bell goes. It's very powerful. After that, everyone says the Academy prayer together. The prayer was written in consultation with students and is also based on the four values. Some students of different faiths or no faith don't want to say the word "God", while some don't want to mention the Trinitarian ending to the prayer. Both those things are fine, just as long as everyone's attention is drawn to the core values.

One of the most challenging aspects of my role is getting the tone right. I don't want to "dumb down" the Christian message, or apologise for it, but at the same time I don't want to come across as "churchy" or "preachy". Many things that work in a church context simply won't work when leading questioning students in worship or reflection. But that keeps me thinking about my faith and the best way to communicate it. It's important to me that our Christian ethos is distinctive yet inclusive.

I see my role as a ministry of presence. Having someone walking around in a clerical collar makes all the difference. I'm not here to preach, or convert or judge anyone, but I might challenge mindsets. Unusually for a school chaplain, I don't have a formal pastoral role, although it's not uncommon for people – both students and teachers – to approach me for pastoral care. Staff will often say something like "I'm not very religious, but will you say a prayer for…"

The Christian character of the school also provides a shape to the school year, with significant Christian celebrations at Christmas and Easter. During Holy Week we take Year 8 and Year 10 to Halifax Minster for a very formal Eucharist. Everybody goes to the front for either a blessing or to receive bread and wine, then they go to the side chapel to light a candle. Afterwards I ask them to give me feedback on the experience and, while it's true that the word "boring" frequently appears on the feedback forms, I am sure that it's an experience that stays with them and enriches them – culturally and socially as well as spiritually. For some it is a really profound experience that they would not otherwise have had. Once, during the service, one girl came and asked me: "Sir, am I supposed to feel like this?" I replied that that depended on how she was feeling, and she burst into tears. As I see it, she had an experience of God.

One of the most moving moments of every year for me is to finish the Year 11 leavers' assembly by pronouncing a blessing from God upon our students.

*Marcus Bull, Chaplain,
Trinity Academy, Halifax*

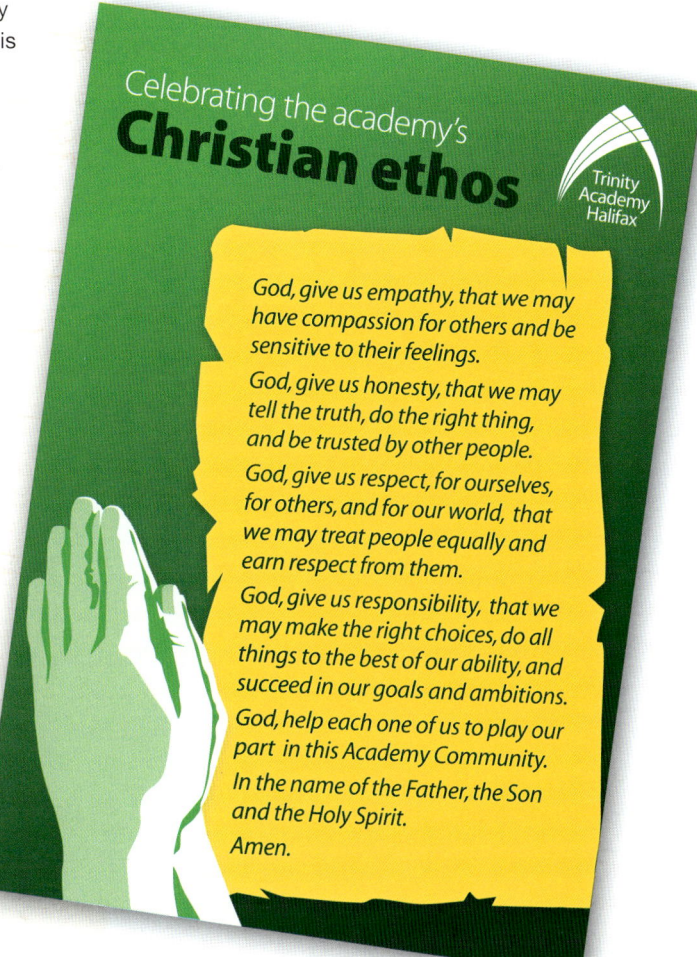

Celebrating the academy's Christian ethos

Trinity Academy Halifax

God, give us empathy, that we may have compassion for others and be sensitive to their feelings.

God, give us honesty, that we may tell the truth, do the right thing, and be trusted by other people.

God, give us respect, for ourselves, for others, and for our world, that we may treat people equally and earn respect from them.

God, give us responsibility, that we may make the right choices, do all things to the best of our ability, and succeed in our goals and ambitions.

God, help each one of us to play our part in this Academy Community.

In the name of the Father, the Son and the Holy Spirit.

Amen.

CHAPTER 6

The Seasons and Traditions of the Anglican Communion

Christians are called to be people of joy and hope, because they know they are loved and have reason to celebrate. The Christian community loves to celebrate, and opportunities come round regularly. Schools generally do this very well, and observe the seasons and feast days in colour, art, music, liturgy (the Church's official form of worship), assemblies, prayer and the classroom.

The Church knows how to teach, and uses signs and symbols as well as words. But it is important that the liturgical life of the Church is seen as part of a joined-up message, backed up by actions and words.

This chapter deals with the Church's yearly cycle and introduces some of the rites, rituals and traditions that are associated with it. Hopefully it will help you to understand what is happening and what is behind it and, importantly, how you can contribute. The main thing is to become familiar with the key times of the year, as well as with some of the practices, and to gain a simple understanding of what they are about. The rest will follow!

Sowerby Village CE (VC) Primary School

CHAPTER 6

The church year

The church year (also known as the liturgical calendar) is made up of seasons, within which are various types of events – commemorations, festivals and feast days. A complex set of rules governs which takes precedence over another. In addition, some have fixed dates, while others can be celebrated on the nearest Sunday. While it may appear confusing at first, the result is that no two years will ever look the same – but each is its own unique and colourful reason to celebrate! A lectionary is a helpful booklet – a kind of diary or year planner for the Church – in which the feasts and festivals have been worked out and are listed together with the Bible readings for each day. You could study the church year for literally years, but the following is a description of some of the main features and terms you may come across.

> ### A NOTE ABOUT LITURGICAL COLOURS
>
> These reflect the mood of the season. White, red, green, purple and gold are the most common you will see. If you see red, for example, at a time other than Pentecost, it generally means that a martyr is being commemorated on that day. Purple is a colour of penitence and is used during Advent and Lent. So in Advent wreaths you may see purple candles surrounding a white candle in the middle.

Advent – purple – late November/early December, ending on 24 December

While most people celebrate the New Year on 1 January, the Church's yearly cycle begins in late November or early December, starting on the first Sunday in Advent.

Most people know that Advent is when we prepare for the coming of Christ as a baby. But many people are surprised to learn that Advent is a penitential season because, as well as preparing for the birth of Jesus, we are thinking about when he will come again.

As penitential seasons, Advent and Lent (see below, and also in the glossary at the back of the book) are times for personal renewal, growth and transformation. Simply put, the Church is calling us to sort ourselves out.

So the message of Advent is strong and positive. God has heard the cry of those who are poor or suffering, and comes. Jesus came to save, heal and reconcile, and we must hear and respond to this call to action in our own lives.

Christmas – white and gold – 25 December to 6 January

At Christmas, Christians celebrate Immanuel, from the Hebrew for "God with us". That, of course, took place in the form of the birth of Jesus. In most churches nowadays, the Christmas season comes to a close after the feast of the Baptism of the Lord, which is held on the Sunday after Epiphany. (Epiphany falls on 6 January, and is when Christians celebrate the coming of the Magi, or wise men, to worship Jesus.)

Originally, however, the season lasted for the whole of January and ended with the feast of Candlemas (2 February), which celebrates Jesus being presented in the Temple. So don't be surprised if there are still signs of Christmas when you return to school after the holiday.

Lent – purple – forty days between Ash Wednesday and Easter Sunday

Lent reminds Christians of the forty days that Jesus spent fasting and praying in the desert before he began his ministry (Matthew 4:1-11). It is when the Church prepares for the greatest of all celebrations – Easter. Because its focus is the lead-up to the death of Jesus, Lent is a serious time when the Church encourages us to pray, fast and abstain, and do something for the good of the community. It begins with Ash Wednesday, when in some schools the chaplain or a visiting priest may offer to put an ash cross on the foreheads of students and staff. Most people are familiar with Shrove Tuesday (Pancake Day), the day before Lent begins. The tradition of eating pancakes arose because people needed to use up the food they would not be eating during the Lenten fast.

Holy Week is the sixth and last week of Lent, and forms a dramatic climax to the period. It is when Christians really focus on the events leading up to the crucifixion of Jesus on Good Friday. Schools might organise special services to allow everyone to reflect on the story of the events during that week.

There are subtle but important variations in the liturgy during Lent. For example, "Alleluia" is not used in worship during Lent.

Easter Day – white and gold – 21 March to 25 April

This is a time of rejoicing and celebrating Christ's resurrection from the dead. It is about the triumph of good over evil, life over death. The mood is very different – and "Alleluia" is again sung and said. Easter Day leads into Eastertide (or Paschaltide), which lasts for fifty days.

Pentecost – red – fifty days after Easter Day

This is another amazing event, when Christians focus on the descent of the Holy Spirit on the apostles (Acts 2:1-12). Red symbolises fire and the Holy Spirit. You may hear Pentecost referred to as Whitsunday, or as the birthday of the Church.

Christian worship

Sunday is the most important day of the Christian week, as it is symbolic of the day when, as the Genesis creation story tells, God rested, having created the world (Genesis 2:2). But Sunday worship is only a small part of the picture, and Christian worship and celebrations take many different forms, including:

- The official services of the Church (liturgy).

- Specially designed services – when the school designs its own style of worship.

- Worship – a general term for giving glory, praise and thanks to God.

- Prayer – listening and speaking to God, either collectively or individually. There are various kinds of prayer, which are outlined below and in the glossary at the back of the book, where you will also find some useful prayers.

CHAPTER 6

The sacraments

The most important Christian rituals are known as the sacraments. The word "sacrament" comes from the Latin *sacramentum*, and came into use in the Church via the Roman army. A recruit became a soldier by taking an oath and being branded! As an initiated soldier, he then had responsibilities, as well as perks to go with them. This double status provided theologians with the model for what they were trying to illustrate when describing the rites of the Church as both spiritual and physical. The person undergoing the sacrament simultaneously receives new responsibilities and a new spiritual status before God. Happily the practice of branding was never used by the Church!

All Anglican churches administer two sacraments – baptism and Eucharist:

- Baptism is where someone (generally when, but by no means always, a baby) is admitted to the Church. The rite involves the use of water.
- The Eucharist – or Holy Communion – is when someone receives the body and blood of Christ in the form of bread and wine. It is seen as an act of unity with the whole Church.

As well as these two sacraments, there are other important rites that it is helpful to be aware of:[1]

- Confirmation is when someone who is considered personally responsible for their faith confirms what was promised by them or on their behalf at baptism.
- Matrimony – or marriage.
- Holy orders refers to the ordination of priests and deacons.

Daily worship and prayer

There is a statutory obligation for a church school to hold a collective act of worship each day, which must be mainly Christian in character. This can be as a whole school, a tutor group or a year group.

As a member of staff you are expected to support the school's prayer life. You may be attached to a class or a tutor group, in which case you will be asked to lead prayer or help pupils do so. If you are not part of any faith group this can appear daunting, but no one is going to assess whether or not you pray, or how "well" you do it. Your task is to create opportunities for people to pray if they choose to.

People pray together or as individuals, and prayers can be said inwardly or recited aloud. They may be spontaneous or follow a written prayer. The Church is rich with a variety of ways of praying. It is helpful to think of the acronym ACTS to remember some of them:

- Adoration – worshipping, praising and adoring God.
- Confession – acknowledging wrongdoing and failings and asking for forgiveness.
- Thanksgiving – offering thanks to God.
- Supplication – praying for ourselves and others.

Near the back of the book you will find guidelines for praying and suggested prayers you can use individually, with colleagues, or with children and young people.

POINTS TO REMEMBER

- The liturgical seasons are wonderful times for focusing and refocusing us on what matters – and cause for celebration!

- The rites and rituals of the Church are a wonderful way of marking the stages of life and deepening our relationship with one another and God.

- Everyone is included in the prayer life of the school.

- Don't be afraid to express yourself creatively within the liturgy. If you have an idea for developing the prayer life of the school, check with someone that it is acceptable – then go for it!

- If you are invited to a baptism or confirmation, seriously consider going, and treat it as an opportunity to celebrate and learn.

- Everyone is on a learning curve in their understanding of the forms of worship and the seasons of the Church. If in doubt, ask for help.

POINTS FOR PERSONAL REFLECTION OR GROUP DISCUSSION

- How does your school celebrate the liturgical year?

- What would help you to develop your understanding of the different forms of worship and their importance?

- How do you feel about leading pupils in prayer? Would you like more training and help? If so, who might you approach?

PRAYER

Creator God, who turns the wheel of the seasons, help us to value the spring, summer, autumn and winter, in all their wonder and beauty.
Help us to deepen our faith through our celebration of the seasons of the Church,
and show us how to pass on the wisdom and joy of the liturgy to the young people in our care.
This we ask in Jesus' name.
Amen.

---

[1] Some Anglicans also use the sacrament of reconciliation, sometimes called confession or penance, and perhaps more familiar as a Roman Catholic sacrament. It is when a person confesses their sins and is forgiven. In other words, through confronting their wrongdoing and saying sorry, they have become reconciled with God. In some traditions, another sacrament, the anointing of the sick, is given when someone is ill or near death. It is also known as healing.

Trinity Academy

CHAPTER 7

Who's Who

You may hear the language of the family used a lot in your school – or if not, it should be – because in a church school you find the family of the Church, or at least a branch of the family tree.

The Church takes its family language all the way back to its teaching of God as our Father and Jesus as his Son. Jesus emphasises this relationship when he refers to God as "Abba" (Mark 14:36) – a term of affection which translates as something like "Dad" or "Daddy".

What's more, we believe we are called to be brothers and sisters to Jesus (see Matthew 12:50) and one another. St Paul certainly thought so, and in his letters to the men and women of the early Church, he frequently addresses his readers as "brothers and sisters" (for example, in Romans 16:17). This is why in some traditions, clergy and people in religious life are known as "Brother", "Sister" or "Father".

Like any family, the Church organises itself into roles, and in the glossary at the back of the book you can find some definitions of who's who and the roles that they play. Some of these you are may meet regularly in the school, while others will visit on special occasions.

The structure of a church school

Who's in charge?

Church schools have a variety of management structures depending on the nature of their foundation. The Diocesan Board of Education has an advisory role and the governors are responsible for the school as a whole. The governing body then delegates the day-to-day running of the school to the headteacher. The Chair of the governing body and the headteacher work closely together to ensure that the school and its teaching reflect its Christian foundation.

Some of the school's senior leaders, heads of department and teachers may be practising Christians. Some may belong to another faith tradition, or to none at all. But what is important is that everyone knows and understands the school mission statement and aims and objectives, and feels able to support them and encourage others to live them out.

The governors

Governors are our unsung heroes – really important people. At the end of the day they are your employer, and are appointed to ensure that the school fulfils its mission and strives for excellence. To carry out their duties to the best of their ability they need to know as much as possible about the school, and have a clear picture of the quality of teaching and learning so that they can support the head. It is not an easy job and it is amazing that so many people are willing to give their time and expertise for free!

The governing body will consist of foundation governors, parent governors, staff governors and local authority governors. As we have seen, foundation governors are appointed by the bishop and have a majority on the governing body. Their role includes a duty to preserve and promote the Christian nature of the school, as described in the ethos statement and trust deed.

You will meet the governors at big events as well as in supporting roles from time to time. For example, in primary schools it's not uncommon for a governor with a particular area of expertise to give one-to-one support in certain areas of the curriculum under the direction of the class teacher. Some will give their time and skills in a wide variety of activities, such as administration, meal times and extracurricular activities.

INTERVIEW – THE MATHS TEACHER

I'm a practising Catholic and although there are differences, I like working in a church school, because it's what I knew growing up. There is a big focus on building relationships with the students here, and to me that's what really matters.

If you have faith, you have to be prepared to model it, because otherwise the kids will question what you're doing. As a form tutor, I can see that not all of the students feel comfortable saying the school prayer, but I don't push for that.

The staff get along well and faith is no barrier to socialising. Sometimes you have to check what's acceptable for someone in their tradition – for example, when we are running a sweepstake! Or when some of us are going out for a meal together, you have to make sure that you're going somewhere where everyone's requirements can be catered for. But that says more to me about how well we get on.

It's great if you can get debates going. We've had some really interesting discussions. It's important to have a mix, because otherwise you're missing out on different perspectives on life.

Katie Dennett, Lead Teacher, Maths, Trinity Academy, Halifax

Jesus – the model of servant leadership

The Gospels contain some very interesting and challenging insights into leadership. When Jesus came to public attention, many people thought that this wonder-worker had come to free Israel from the tyranny of Roman occupation. But Jesus was not an avenging liberator. Instead, he turned conventional wisdom on its head and redefined leadership in ways we are still trying to come to terms with.

In Mark's Gospel (10:43) Jesus tells his disciples James and John, "whoever wishes to become great among you must be your servant" – something he lived out in his ministry. Here are two more examples from the Bible, of Jesus demonstrating "servant leadership":

Jesus enters Jerusalem
This passage tells the story of how Jesus entered Jerusalem. By this point he had huge crowds following him everywhere he went. But Jesus refused to make it a triumphal procession and instead rode on a humble donkey, deliberately making the point that his mission is nothing to do with domination, power games or show. For all that, however, the crowd recognised him for who he was – their excitement comes through loud and clear in the Bible story!

Luke 19:28-40

Jesus washes the disciples' feet
In John's account of the Last Supper, Jesus washes the feet of his disciples. This task was usually performed by a slave, who had the less than pleasant job of cleaning guests' feet. It really wasn't something you would volunteer to do, which is why the disciples were so appalled when Jesus did it. What was he playing at? They recoiled at his show of humility but Jesus insisted, in order to teach them something about his kind of leadership.

John 13:1-17

The servants of the servants of God

No organisation can exist without a degree of authority or accountability – we would simply be left with a complete free-for-all. Servant leadership is about how this authority is used. Jesus didn't spend time drawing up rules and regulations, but he often spoke with authority (Mark 1:22). It is more to do with *truth* than with the desire to control and dominate. In the Church, we look to the leaders to speak with authority, while at the same being examples of humble service.

In our schools, we should be looking for much the same thing, although of course the reality is that you will find as many different models of leadership as there are leaders. Like any community, the Church goes through phases when its foundational beliefs are strong, and other times when they are challenged. There have been times in the life of the Church when the clergy have striven to emulate Jesus' example of servant leadership, and other times when power has gone to people's heads.

Some of the leaders you encounter in your work may be clear examples of servant leadership while others… well, let's not be too hard on them. It's not easy being a leader in a modern church school – which is why we pray for our leaders!

POINTS TO REMEMBER

- We all have an important role in the family.
- The clergy are here to serve, and want to. As humans, however, we all fail – so if you find someone falling short of the mark, have the courage to discuss it with them.
- The Church needs you!

POINTS FOR PERSONAL REFLECTION OR GROUP DISCUSSION

- What do you think and feel about the model of servant leadership?
- To what degree, if any, do you feel part of the family?
- As a learning community, how do you feel you can grow closer to the family model?

PRAYER

Loving God,
Grant me your hope, that I may know the value of living.
Grant me your strength, that I may have courage whatever happens.
Grant me your patience, that I pause before I judge.
Grant me your wisdom, that I discover how to learn from the children.
Grant me your mercy, that I may temper my discipline.
Grant me your peace, that I may become an instrument of reconciliation.
And in all things flood me in your joy that I may keep alight the flame of your love.
Amen.

CHAPTER 8

Guidance for Praying and Suggestions for Prayers

Time to pray

When a group gathers together – believers and non-believers alike, for whatever purpose – it is very helpful to take a few moments at the beginning to pause and centre as a group, focusing on the task ahead and putting aside other preoccupations. Similarly, at the end of a meeting or class, a short prayer consolidates and strengthens what has been discussed and any decisions that have been made.

This chapter is designed as a resource to help you develop your prayer life, as an individual, as a group of colleagues, or with students.

Many non-Christians are happy to share in a time of prayer even if they do not subscribe to the sentiments expressed, although others may be less comfortable. One solution is to invite people to use the time to reflect on the work you are about to do and the wider concerns of this school.

If a substantial proportion of the school community belongs to another faith, it may be appropriate to include a prayer from another faith community, such as the traditional Jewish Sabbath prayer over children, given on the facing page, which is based on a passage from the Old Testament (Numbers 6:22-27).

> Do not forget to say your prayers. If your prayer is sincere, there will be every time you pray a new feeling containing an idea in it, an idea you did not know before, which will give fresh courage: you will then understand that prayer is education.
>
> *Fyodor Dostoevsky*

Ye'varech'echa Adonoy ve'yish'merecha.
Ya'ir Adonoy panav eilecha viy-chuneka.
Yisa Adonoy panav eilecha, ve'yasim lecha shalom.

This translates as:

May God bless you and watch over you.
May God shine his face towards you and show you favour.
May God look on you with favour and grant you shalom peace.[1]

Or the Muslim prayer:

O my Lord, dispose me that I may be thankful for
Thy blessing with which Thou hast blessed me and
my father and mother and that I may do righteousness,
well-pleasing to Thee and make me righteous
… surely I turn to Thee and
surely I am of those who submit.[2]

Trinity Academy

What should prayers consist of?

One model for opening prayers is that recommended by Prebendary Sam Wells in his guide to leading public prayers.[3] This examines the "time-honoured shape", or archetypal prayer in the Anglican tradition – the collect. A well-known example is the Collect for Purity, which has five elements:

1. The address to God – "Almighty God", "God the healer".
2. The context in which God has been active and an explanation of why the person praying (on behalf of all those present) believes that God will listen and respond.
3. What precisely it is that those praying want God to do.
4. The outcome in terms of the change to the community.
5. The conclusion, shaping the prayer in light of the invocation of the Trinity.

So a prayer at the beginning of a meeting of teachers following this pattern may be along the following lines:

> God who protects and teaches,
> who gave a practical example of teaching through the parables,
> guide and strengthen us,
> that we may always act in the best interests of all for whom we are responsible.
> Through Jesus Christ our Lord, who lives and reigns with you in the unity of the Holy Spirit, one God, now and for ever.
> Amen.

An intercessory prayer (for more about this, see the glossary) can be responsorial – with everyone saying a petition or response together after each line or verse. For example, the line: "Lord, in your mercy" might be responded to with: "Hear our prayer".

A meeting could end with a well-known and trusted prayer that most people will know, such as the Lord's Prayer or the Grace, both of which are based on Bible verses:

THE LORD'S PRAYER

Our Father in heaven,
hallowed be your name,
your kingdom come,
your will be done,
on earth as in heaven.
Give us today our daily bread.
Forgive us our sins
as we forgive those who sin against us.
Lead us not into temptation
but deliver us from evil.
For the kingdom, the power,
and the glory are yours
now and for ever.
Amen.

Based on Matthew 6:9-15

THE GRACE

May the grace of our Lord Jesus Christ,
and the love of God,
and the fellowship of the Holy Spirit,
be with us all, evermore.
Amen.

Based on 2 Corinthians 13:13

CHAPTER 8

Love to pray – feel the need to pray often through the day and take the trouble to pray. If you want to pray better, you must pray more. Prayer enlarges the heart until it is capable of containing God's gift of himself. Ask and seek and your heart will grow big enough to receive him and keep him as your own.

Mother Teresa[5]

God will always answer our prayers; but He will answer them in His way, and His way will be the way of perfect wisdom and of perfect love. Often if He answered our prayers as we at that moment desire, it would be the worst thing possible for us, for in our ignorance we often ask for gifts which would be our ruin.

William Barclay[4]
Minister, radio & television presenter
(1907 – 1978)

Prayer takes place in the heart, not in the head.

Carlo Carretto[6]
(1910 – 1988)

Prayers for different occasions

A PRAYER FOR THE START OF THE SCHOOL YEAR

God of love and mercy, we praise you for the wonder of our being, for all that you have created us to be.
Guide us, both staff and students, as we begin a new school year.
Bless each one of us with your strength and grace as we grow in wisdom and knowledge, searching to understand the mystery and wonder of your creation.
We ask this through Jesus Christ our Lord.
Amen.

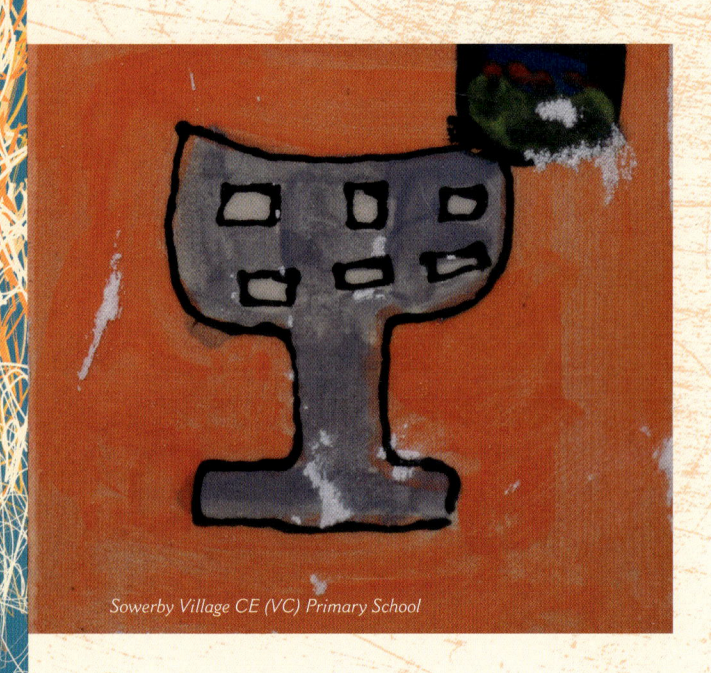

Sowerby Village CE (VC) Primary School

A PRAYER FOR THE NEW SCHOOL YEAR

All: Come, Holy Spirit!
Come into our school at the start of the year.
Enlighten our minds to your work:
… in us;
… through us;
… for us.
May we all become the channel of your love for our community.

All: Come, Holy Spirit!
Help us to be people of courage:
… to challenge;
… to change;
… to transform.
So that we may be renewed in our commitment to build the kingdom of God.

All: Come, Holy Spirit!
Come into our gathering at the start of this school year.
Open our hearts to you, speaking:
… in our colleagues;
… through our children and young people;
… in our governors.
Inspire us to be a people of hope.

All: Come, Holy Spirit!
Enlighten the eyes of our minds:
… to see you in people who challenge us;
… to know you working in situations we don't understand;
… to perceive you moving gently in our hearts.
Help us to be people of wisdom.
Amen.

CHAPTER 8

A PRAYER FOR WISDOM AND UNDERSTANDING
Teach me, O my Lord Jesus,
instruct me that I may learn from Thee
what I ought to teach concerning thee.

Archbishop William Land
(1573 – 1645)

A PRAYER FOR WILLINGNESS TO SERVE OTHERS
Lord, make us instruments of your peace.
Where there is hatred, let us sow love;
where there is injury, pardon;
where there is discord, union;
where there is doubt, faith;
where there is despair, hope;
where there is darkness, light;
where there is sadness, joy.
Grant that we may not so much seek
to be consoled as to console;
to be understood as to understand;
to be loved as to love.
For it is in giving that we receive;
it is in pardoning that we are pardoned;
and it is in dying that we are born to eternal life.
Amen.

St Francis of Assisi

A PRAYER FOR GOD'S INSPIRATION
Father, may everything we do
begin with your inspiration
and continue with your saving help.
Let our work always find its origin in you
and through you reach completion.
We ask this through our Lord Jesus Christ, your Son,
who lives and reigns with you and the Holy Spirit,
one God, for ever and ever.
Amen.

The Liturgy of the Hours

A PRAYER FOR CHILDREN AND YOUNG PEOPLE
Loving God,
your Son told his disciples
to become like little children.
Lead us to work for the welfare
and protection of all young people.
May we respect their dignity
that they may flourish in life,
following the example of the same
Jesus Christ our Lord.
Amen.[7]

A PRAYER FOR STUDENTS BEFORE SATs
Father of all our children, enlighten and encourage each child here today as they do their tests.
We bless you for each one and thank you for the gift that they are for us.
May they be able to recall all that you have helped us to teach them and feel proud of their achievements.
Amen.

A PRAYER BEFORE STUDENTS SIT THEIR FINAL EXAMINATIONS

O Lord, help our students as they sit their examinations, to recall the things which they have learned and studied.

May they remember clearly and set down that which they know so well.

Steady their nerves and calm their minds, doing justice to all their hard work.

May each one feel that they have achieved the very best they can be.

Amen.

A PRAYER FOR THE END OF TERM

Christ, our Teacher,
bless everyone in our school
as we come to the end of the year.
Pour out your loving grace
on all who have given so much,
asking only that each one may receive
that which you have prepared for them.
We give thanks for everyone in the school
for this year of nurturing and growth,
of laughter, of fun, of joy of discovery.
We give thanks for the challenges and
achievements, for the hard times, the
misunderstandings and the joy of forgiveness.
Stay with us in our rest days,
so that we may be renewed and restored.
Keep each one safe in your loving embrace
so that we may return renewed to continue
the ongoing discovery of your love.
Amen.

PRAYER IN TIMES OF TROUBLE

I asked for strength that I might achieve;
I was made weak that I might learn humbly to obey.
I asked for health that I might do greater things;
I was given infirmity that I might do better things.
I asked for riches that I might be happy;
I was given poverty that I might be wise.
I asked for power that I might have the praise of men;
I was given weakness that I might feel the need of God.
I asked for all things that I might enjoy life;
I was given life that I might enjoy all things.
I got nothing that I had asked for,
but everything that I had hoped for.
Almost despite myself my unspoken prayers were answered;
I am, among all men, most richly blessed.
Amen.

Attributed to an unknown Confederate soldier

A PRAYER FOR TIMES OF REJOICING

O come, let us sing to the Lord;
let us make a joyful noise to the rock of our salvation!
Let us come into his presence with thanksgiving;
let us make a joyful noise to him with songs of praise!
For the Lord is a great God, and a great King above all gods.
In his hand are the depths of the earth; the heights of the mountains are his also.
The sea is his, for he made it, and the dry land, which his hands have formed.
O come, let us worship and bow down, let us kneel before the Lord, our Maker!
For he is our God, and we are the people of his pasture, and the sheep of his hand.
Amen.

Psalm 95:1-7

CHAPTER 8

A WELSH-LANGUAGE PRAYER
GWEDDI DYDD G YL DEWI

Diolch, diolch am Gymru, diolch am wlad, am dir, am iaith.
Diolch, diolch am Iesu, am ei gariad, am ei waith;
dyma weddi Dydd G yl Dewi, de a gogledd,
cenwch gan:
boed i'r Cymry garu'r Iesu cadwn Gymru'n Gymru lan.
Amen.

This translates as:

ST DAVID'S DAY PRAYER

Thank you, thank you for Wales.
Thank you for our country, land and language.
Thank you, thank you for Jesus,
for his love and his work;
this is a St David's Day prayer,
north and south, sing this song:
let us in Wales love Jesus
and keep our country holy.
Amen.

POINTS FOR PERSONAL REFLECTION OR GROUP DISCUSSION

- What part does prayer play in your ministry as a member of staff?
- How comfortable are you with praying together with other staff and students?
- Is there anything you would prefer not to say in prayer?
- Are there resources which might help you grow in prayer?
- How do you think you could help the wider school community in their understanding and growth in prayer?

1 Quoted in Mark Herringshaw, "*A Hebrew Blessing for Children*": www.beliefnet.com
2 Surah Al-Ahqaf, verse 15[1].
3 Samuel Wells, *Crafting Prayers for Public Worship* (Norwich: Canterbury Press, 2013).
4 William Barclay, *The Gospel of Matthew* (Edinburgh: St Andrew Press, 1956).
5 Quoted in *Mother Teresa: In the silence of the heart*, edited by Kathryn Spink (Oxford: Isis, 1985).
6 Carlo Carretto, *The Desert in the City* (London: Fount, 1981).
7 The Church of England/Prayers for Children and Families, at: www.churchofengland.org

A GLOSSARY OF CHRISTIAN TERMS

The following list is by no means exhaustive, but it includes many words and phrases you may well come across.

A

Advent: The season of the Church's year leading up to Christmas. It includes the four Sundays before Christmas and it is a time of preparation for the "coming" of Christ. Advent marks the beginning of the Church's year.

All Saints' Day: The day on which Christians remember all the saints of the Church, celebrated on 1 November.

All Souls' Day: The day on which Christians remember and pray for those who have died, observed on 2 November.

Altar: In a church, the table on which the Eucharist (see below) is celebrated.

Angel: The word means "messenger". In the Bible they are described as carrying messages from God to human beings.

Anglican Communion: A collection of Churches in the Anglican tradition. For a more in-depth explanation, turn to Chapter Two.

Annunciation: The announcement by the angel Gabriel to Mary that she was to be the mother of the Messiah. It is celebrated on 25 March.

Anointing of the sick: Anointing a sick person with oil for healing.

Apostles: The twelve men who were Jesus' closest followers. Known as disciples while he was on earth, they are referred to as apostles after his ascension to his Father.

Apostolate: The work of an apostle. It is used to describe any work, ministry or service which is carried out on behalf of the Church. For example, the apostolate of a religious order is the work the order undertakes.

Archbishop: The chief bishop responsible for a large district (or archdiocese). There are two archdioceses in England (York and Canterbury) and one in Wales.

Ascension: The taking up of Jesus into heaven forty days after the resurrection, witnessed by the apostles. Ascension Day is celebrated on a Thursday, forty days after Easter.

Ash Wednesday: The first day of Lent. By tradition Christians have ashes put on their foreheads on this day as a mark of repentance. It may also be a day of fasting.

GLOSSARY

B

Baptism: The rite by which a person (generally, but by no means always, a baby) is admitted to the Church. The rite involves the use of water.

Benefice: Parishes that are linked together in some way, often under one incumbent (see below). This has been a trend in recent years, where parishes have been amalgamated as a cost-saving measure.

Bible: The collective name for the set of books or scriptures that form the Old and New Testaments.

Bidding prayers: Prayers said during a church service for the needs of the Church and the world.

Bishop: A priest who is entrusted with a position of authority and oversight over other clergy and laity. A diocesan bishop oversees a diocese – an administrative geographical area – and may be assisted by assistant or suffragan bishops.

Blessing: A short prayer, usually accompanied by the sign of the cross, asking God's favour on persons or objects.

Body of Christ: The collective term for all Christian believers, or the wafer or bread after it has been consecrated at the Eucharist (see below).

Book of Common Prayer: The original service book of the Church of England. It is still in use, but a more recent service book, *Common Worship*, is used for many services. Most Anglican Communion churches have a version of the *Book of Common Prayer*.

C

Candlemas: The feast which commemorates the presentation of Jesus in the Temple by Mary and Joseph. It is held on 2 February, the fortieth day in the Christmas period.

Canon: An honorary title conferred upon a member of the clergy (and occasionally a lay person) for faithful and valuable service to the Church.

Cathedral: The principal church of a diocese, with which the bishop is officially associated.

Chalice: The cup used at the Eucharist (see below) to hold the wine.

Chaplain: A member of the clergy who is attached to a private chapel or an institution (such as the Armed Forces, a school, a prison or a hospital).

Chapter: The governing body of a cathedral or other religious community.

Charismatic renewal: A movement within the Church which aims for renewal by being attuned to the power of the Holy Spirit working in the lives of individuals and communities.

Chrism: A mixture of olive oil and balsam which is blessed by the bishop on Maundy Thursday and used in baptism, confirmation and ordination.

Christian Church: A term used to refer to worldwide Christianity. Within that, there are other individual Churches (such as the Church of England and the Church in Wales).

Christmas: The feast of the birth of Jesus, celebrated on 25 December.

Christ the King: A feast celebrated on the last Sunday of the Church's year acclaiming Christ as king of the world.

Clergy: A term applied to men and women who have been ordained for ministry within the Church. Bishops, priests and deacons are members of the clergy.

Common Worship: The most recent Church of England service book.

Confirmation: The rite in which someone who is considered personally responsible for their faith confirms what was promised either by them or on their behalf at their baptism.

Contrition: The acknowledgement of sin and sorrow for it.

Convent: The place where a community of nuns lives.

Corpus Christi: A Latin phrase meaning "the Body of Christ". The feast of Corpus Christi commemorates the institution of the Eucharist (see below) and is celebrated on the Thursday after Trinity Sunday.

Creed: A summary of Christian beliefs.

Crucifix: A cross with the figure of the crucified Jesus upon it, used by Christians to bring to mind the sufferings of Christ.

Curate: A member of the clergy engaged as assistant to a vicar, rector or parish priest. This will often be someone who has been ordained, but has not yet been installed as the incumbent (see below) of a parish or benefice.

D

Deacon: There are two types of deacon. One is the "transitional" deacon – someone who has been ordained as a deacon as the final stage of preparation to be ordained as a priest (they normally remain a deacon for about a year). The other type is the "permanent" or "distinctive" deacon, ordained by the bishop to that role, who will remain a deacon and not be ordained a priest.

Deanery: Several parishes form a deanery. This unit is administered by one of the priests of the deanery who has the title "Dean".

Devil: The biblical name for the evil one, a creature who rebelled against God and causes evil.

Diocese: An area under the care of a bishop.

Disciples: Refers to Jesus' twelve companions while he was on earth, but may also be used of anyone who follows him.

Doctrines: What Christians believe, expressed in the Creed and other official documents.

E

Easter: The day on which Christians celebrate the resurrection of Jesus.

Ecumenism: The work for unity between the different Christian traditions.

GLOSSARY

Epiphany: The feast which commemorates the visit of the wise men to the infant Christ in Bethlehem. It is celebrated on 6 January.

Episcopal/ian: The term "Episcopalian" refers to someone who believes that a Church should be governed by bishops. In Scotland, Christians in the Anglican tradition belong to the Scottish Episcopal Church, while the mainstream Anglican Communion in the USA is known as the Episcopal Church in the United States of America (ECUSA).

Eucharist: The last time Jesus ate with his disciples (see "Last Supper"), he symbolically enacted the breaking up of his body (as bread) and the spilling of his blood (as wine) – a powerful gesture which Christians remember and re-enact when they share bread and wine at a form of worship known as Holy Communion (see below).

F

Fasting: Eating less food than usual as an act of self-denial.

Feast day: A day of special celebration within the Church.

Font: A basin or bowl in a church used for the baptismal water. In Anglican churches fonts are often historical stone structures.

G

Godparent: Someone who undertakes to ensure that a child who is baptised will be brought up in the Christian faith.

Good Friday: The day on which the crucifixion of Jesus is commemorated.

Gospel: A word meaning "good news". The proclamation of the good news of salvation won for us by Jesus Christ. The word is also used of the four books which tell of the life, death and resurrection of Jesus – the Gospels of Matthew, Mark, Luke and John.

Grace at meals: A short prayer before and after meals, thanking God for the food we eat and asking God's blessing on those who have prepared it.

H

Habit: The distinctive form of dress worn by members of religious communities.

Holy Communion: The service that re-enacts the Last Supper (see below). Also known as the Eucharist or the Mass.

Holy orders: This term refers either to the three ordained orders of deacon, priest and bishop, or to the rite by which they are ordained.

Holy Trinity: The Christian doctrine that there is one God in three persons: Father, Son and Holy Spirit. It is generally acknowledged to be a very difficult teaching to begin to comprehend! Indeed it is, and always will be, pure mystery.

Holy Week: The final week of Lent, leading up to Easter Sunday. The last three days of Holy Week (Maundy Thursday, Good Friday and Easter Saturday or Easter Eve) are days of special solemnity.

Host: The wafer of consecrated bread which Christians receive at Holy Communion. It is usually disc-shaped and thin for convenience, and there are two sizes – the larger is used by the priest at the altar. Some churches use a loaf of bread in place of wafers.

I

Incarnation: A theological term for the Son of God becoming man in Jesus Christ.

Incumbent: The holder of an office or post. In the Church this term is often used to refer to a parish priest, vicar or rector.

Intercession: Prayers offered on behalf of others, sometimes called "petitionary prayer" (bidding prayers fall into this category).

J

Jesus: There are a number of symbols for the name Jesus which you may see in churches or works of religious art. These are some of them:

- *ICHTHYS*: an acrostic consisting of the initial letters of five Greek words, forming the Greek word for fish. These five words represent the divine character of Jesus: *Iesous* (Jesus), *Christos* (Christ), *Theou* (God's), *Yios* (Son), *Soter* (Saviour).
- *IHS*: three letters from the Greek name, Jesus.
- *INRI*: the initial letters from the Latin inscription written on the cross: "*Iesus Nazarenus Rex Iudaeorum*" (Jesus of Nazareth, King of the Jews).
- *PX*: a monogram of the first two Greek letters for "Christos".

Joseph: The husband of Mary, venerated as a saint. His feast is celebrated on 19 March.

K

Kyrie Eleison: Greek words meaning "Lord have mercy". Sometimes said or sung in Greek during Holy Communion.

L

Laity: Members of the Church who do not belong to the clergy or a religious order.

Last Supper: The supper Jesus had with his disciples on the night before he died, during which he introduced them to the practice of the Eucharist (see above).

Lectern: The stand from which the scriptures are read in church.

Lectionary: A book containing the Bible readings for the year.

Lent: A period of six weeks leading up to Easter, symbolic of the forty days that Jesus spent in the wilderness. It begins on Ash Wednesday and is a time of self-denial in preparation for Easter. Many Christians choose some form of self-denial or abstinence during Lent.

Liturgical year: The worship of the Church over the period of a year during which the central mysteries of faith are unfolded. The chief festivals are Christmas, Easter and Pentecost.

GLOSSARY

Liturgy: The formal public worship of the Church.

Lord's Prayer: The prayer Jesus taught his followers to say. It starts with the words: "Our Father in heaven" (see page 68 for the full version).

M

Martyr: A Christian who bears witness to the truth of the Gospel to the point of death.

Mass: The service that re-enacts the Last Supper (see above). Also known as the Eucharist or Holy Communion.

Maundy Thursday: The Thursday in Holy Week (see above). Jesus ate the Last Supper with his disciples on this day.

Missionaries: Christians who proclaim the Gospel to non-Christians. It is also often applied to anyone who endeavours to share his or her faith with others.

N

New Testament: That part of the Bible which tells the Good News of Jesus Christ.

Non-stipendiary: Non-stipendiary ministers or priests do not receive payment for their services.

O

Old Testament: That part of the Bible written before the time of Christ.

Ordination: The conferring of holy orders on someone, by which he or she becomes a bishop, priest or deacon.

P

Palm Sunday: The Sunday before Easter. It commemorates the occasion when Jesus rode into Jerusalem on a donkey and the people waved palm branches in his honour. It is also known as Passion Sunday.

Parables: The stories Jesus told which illustrate some of his most important teachings.

Paradise: Another word for heaven. It literally means "God's garden", and so is also used of the Garden of Eden.

Parish: The community of the Church in a particular place.

Parochial Church Council (PCC): A group of people elected by the parish who, together with the parish priest, look after various needs of the parish.

Passion: The suffering and death of Jesus on the cross, endured for our salvation.

Passion Sunday: See "Palm Sunday", above.

Pastoral care: The caring work of the Church, particularly that exercised by ordained ministers. "Pastor" means "shepherd".

Pentecost: Literally means "fifty days". It marks the day when the Holy Spirit came upon the apostles, fifty days after the resurrection of Jesus. Also called Whit Sunday.

Petition: Asking God for our needs in prayer.

Pilgrimage: A journey to a holy place.

Preaching: Gospel teaching.

Protestantism: The group of Reformed Churches that arose as a result of the Reformation (see below).

R

Rector: A parish priest may be known as a rector, a vicar or a priest in charge, depending on the parish. Historically, a rector received tithes (a kind of tax, which was paid either in money or produce) from the people of the parish, whereas in the case of a vicar, these were passed to another body or individual, but this distinction no longer exists.

Reformation: A movement for the reform of certain doctrines and practices of the Church which began in the sixteenth century and led to the division between Catholic and Protestant (or Reformed) Churches.

Responsorial psalm: A psalm which is recited or sung, during which the congregation recites or sings a response after each verse.

S

Sacrament: A ceremonial rite which imparts spiritual grace – for example, baptism (see above).

Sacrament of the sick: See "anointing of the sick", above.

Saints: People whose holiness of life is recognised after death. The process of recognising a saint is called canonisation. The Anglican tradition does not make saints, but recognises many who were made in other traditions.

Scriptures: The sacred writings of the Bible.

Sermon: A talk in which the word of God is explained. Also called a homily. Only people who have been commissioned by the bishop are allowed to give sermons – usually priests or deacons.

Sign of the cross: A formula some Christians use to bless themselves, often during worship. It is made with the right hand by touching the forehead, the breast and the shoulders, often while saying the words: "In the name of the Father and of the Son and of the Holy Spirit. Amen."

Sin: A rejection of God and the refusal to accept God's love.

Soul: The spiritual element of a person's nature.

Stations of the cross: A series of meditations on incidents in the suffering and death of Christ. Pictures of these scenes can be found round the walls of some churches.

Synod: Within the Anglican Communion, a governing body is known as a synod. There are synods at various levels – for example, a deanery synod, a diocesan synod and the General Synod of the Church of England and Church in Wales. Within a synod there are usually representatives from clergy and laity (see above) and sometimes, depending on the scope of its jurisdiction, from the bishops.

T

Ten Commandments: The rules of life delivered by God to Moses on Mount Sinai. They still form the basis of morality for Christians.

GLOSSARY

Theological college: A college where men and women are trained for the priesthood.

Theology: The study of things concerned with Christian faith and leading a Christian life.

Trinity Sunday: The Sunday after Pentecost. A day on which special honour is paid to the Holy Trinity (see above).

V

Vestments: Garments worn by the ministers of the Church. These include:

- *alb* – a long white tunic worn when celebrating the Eucharist (see above).
- *cassock* – a long black garment worn at non-Eucharistic services.
- *chasuble* – the main outer garment worn by the priest when celebrating Holy Communion (see above).
- *stole* – a type of scarf.
- *surplice* – a white garment worn over a cassock.

Vestry: The room in the church where the priest's garments and vessels are kept.

Vicar: See "Rector", above.

Vocation: The calling to a life of love, service and holiness which is addressed to all Christians. The word is also commonly used in a narrower sense to refer to the calling to the priesthood or religious life.

Vows: Solemn promises of poverty, chastity and obedience which are made by members of religious orders. They can be temporary (binding only for a time) or perpetual (binding for life).

W

Whit Sunday: Another name for the feast of Pentecost (see above), which celebrates the coming of the Holy Spirit on the apostles. "Whit" means "white". In earlier times the newly baptised wore the white robes of baptism on this day.

FURTHER READING AND RESOURCES

Further reading

This is Our Faith: a popular presentation of Anglican belief, by R. Gallagher, J. Trenchard & J. John (Chawton: Redemptorist Publications, 2014). A straightforward explanation of the Christian faith, the Church and worship, written from an Anglican perspective.

Trinity Academy, Halifax

Useful websites

About the Church

The Anglican Communion
www.anglicancommunion.org

The Church of England
www.churchofengland.org

The Church in Wales
www.churchinwales.org.uk

Anglicans Online
www.anglicansonline.org

Christian organisations

Christian Aid
www.christianaid.org.uk

Church Action on Poverty
www.church-poverty.org.uk

Church schools and education

The Church of England Education
www.churchofengland.org/education.aspx

The Church in Wales Schools
www.churchinwales.org.uk/life/schools

Church Schools Cymru
www.churchschoolscymru.org

RESOURCES

The Association for Christian Teachers (ACT)
www.christian-teachers.org.uk
A wide range of online resources to support Christian teachers and governors in both C of E and C in W schools, and secular schools.

The National Society for Promoting Religious Education
www.christianvalues4schools.co.uk
Established in 1811 by Joshua Watson (see Chapter Three) to provide schools for poor children. Today it administers the SIAMS (Statutory Inspection of Anglican and Methodist Schools) inspection of church schools.

Bible resources

Crosswalk.com
http://www.crosswalk.com
A very easy way to access most translations of the Bible.

Prayer resources

Pray for Schools
www.prayforschools.org/resources/group-resources/inspirational-prayers
Encouraging Christians to hold events to increase prayer for schools in their area.

Faith and Worship
www.faithandworship.com/prayers
A personal collection of prayers written by John Birch to be used in private and public worship.

The Franciscans
www.franciscans.org.uk/franciscan-praying/prayers-of-saint-francis

Sacred Space
www.sacredspace.ie
A very useful site which offers a daily time of meditation that is simple yet challenging.

Taizé
http://www.taize.fr/en
A Christian community in France which provides prayer, musical and meditation resources.

Trinity Academy, Halifax